Dark Psychology

How to Use and Recognize Manipulation, Mind Control, and Persuasion to Achieve Goals

By Jennifer Arlington

Copyright @2019

Table of Contents

Chapter 1: Dark Psychology 4

Chapter 2: The New Definition of Black 6

Chapter 3: Really Knowing Your Dark Side 8

Chapter 4: The Definition of Machiavellianism 10

Chapter 5: Control and Manipulation 15

Chapter 6: Empathy 19

Chapter 7: Self-Sabotage 33

Chapter 8: Our Conscience and Moral Decisions 46

Chapter 9: The Craziest, Psychopathic Serial Killers of All Time 49

Chapter 10: How to Identify A Manipulator 53

Chapter 11: How to Outsmart A Master Manipulator 58

Chapter 12: Scams on the Web 61

Chapter 13: Blackmail Tactics 65

Chapter 14: Neuro-Linguistic Programming (NLP) 90

Chapter 15: The Seductive Character 97

Chapter 16: The strategies sex traffickers use to find victims 108

Why does psychological perception of any threat cause physical reactions? The answer is in human anatomy, more precisely, in the reasons of pain appearing. Is mental pain similar to physical pain? How does strong pain happen? With physical real pain, every little thing is ☐uite clear. We do not take into consideration easy motor reflexes that are performed under control of spinal cord.

During physical receptor experience, the nervous impulse is transferred via nerves to corresponding brain part, then the brain sends a response impulse to an organ.

How does mental strong pain happen? Our body has such feature as self-regulation of all physiological procedures, in other words, brain responses on the change in the chemical processes in the body.

Most likely, under the impact of feelings in the body takes place some type of change, for instance, in blood structure, then it is transmitted to the brain, and again the reaction impulse from the brain is sent to among the organs and thus pain happens. This is called the mental reason for the real pain.

For instance, when you fear darkness you could experience distress or discomfort in the throat. You feel like someone stops your breathing. Here you fear not darkness itself but something that can be there in the darkness. It is based upon gotten info about it throughout your life. A little child never ever fears the darkness until he or she is being told what can be in it. Let us call it conscious worry.

Such phobias as fear of a concrete situation or object, that frightens you with something and produces a feeling of fear and horror, are also referred to as conscious worry as you feel this fear because of your bad experience or negative information received from someone else. What is the nature of this fear? How does this worry happen? What do I feel? Lack of confidence, embarrassment, dejection, lack of exercise, anxiety, blame, injury, consternation, stress, and panic.

There are mental and physical feelings in your body. And that means that worry is adjoined with other negative emotions. Just one thing causes another, and originates from the other, but means one and the exact same thing.

What about unconscious worry or, in other words, a simple fear not based upon this experience? What can it be? This can be the fear of the uncertainty, or the fear of the unidentified. For instance, kids fear noises, unidentified things. Generally, from the very start of human history, people were always scared of inexplicable acts of nature. Or their worry was based on a phenomenon seen right before.

For example, fear of the unidentified future, fear of possible thought negative events. How do we discover that these are bad events? We compare possible events with skilled negative ones.

It ends up that we fear unknown things since we fear bad unidentified things. We do not fear good unknown things since they make us happy. And when we feel fear, all good events we do forget. In other words, when we think of an unidentified event in our mind a threatening image appears, as a result, occurs some feeling of worry based upon negative early knowledgeable worry. It means that fear of an unknown thing is a conscious worry.

Black is not a color as such. Color is light and black is devoid of light. Actually, it takes in light, reflecting nothing back. It is, therefore, warmer than white, which shows all colors, retaining none. Although both black and white aren't colors, as agents of lightness and darkness, they are responsible for all the beautiful hues we see around us.

Psychologically, black is related to overall darkness and with the unidentified. It is the opposite of white. Whereas black is typically connected with wickedness, white represents light, purity, and goodness. In fact, both have their positive and negative sides. White represents sunlight. This light not only gives us heat and brightens up the spirit but, when the rays of light are too extreme, can lead to loss of sight. On the other hand, darkness makes every little thing invisible and subsequently causes worry. Yet it is the darkness of meditation that allows us to become silent and focused, in order to discover the inner truth, the inner light.

Black and white are actually inseparable. As agents for light and darkness, they form an absolute polarity. As soon as the light is snuffed out, darkness happens and when light appears, darkness disappears.

Like every hue, black has two very conflicting qualities. Its negative side represents shame, anxiety, heaviness and, at its extreme, evilness. Positively, it represents stability, concentration, depth, weight, power, and exclusivity. It is mystical with endless depth. Those who do not fear this will experience black as highly spiritual; those who fear these qualities will see it as harmful and wicked.

Black is used to expressing the fearful and the mystical. It means exclusivities or class, such as for the black limousine or the black evening gown. It is certainly the favorite color for signifying luxury and eminence. Its tremendous depth gives it a powerful attraction.

CONQUERING YOUR WORRY OF DARKNESS USING HYPNOSIS

Being afraid of the dark is not something that one must be humiliated by. Self-hypnosis is a practice that can provide a person with an escape of the immobilizing fear. It does so in 3 ways:

1. Comprehending the worry

To treat this fear of darkness, one should first understand it. Fear of the dark is an inherent human characteristic that goes way back to prehistoric times. In essence, being conscious enough not to stray in the dark has kept tons of the people in ancient times safe. The reason for this is that man doesn't have the capability to see clearly in the dark, leaving people vulnerable to many predators, especially in the wild.

The problem with this fear is that the majority of the modern security measures have rendered most hassles found in the dark invalid. If your place is safe enough, then being afraid of the dark is unproven and ☐uite problematic. In many cases today, the fear of the dark focuses on fictional specters and creatures that are thought of to be looming around dark corners.

2. Returning

The fear of darkness is mental in nature and therefore must be treated like a serious phobia in hypnosis sessions. A lot of phobias connected to darkness are caused by deep mental trauma in the past, particularly during childhood. A hypnotherapy session will have you recall those memories which activated your worry

The reason for revisiting the memories is to let you experience them once again, but, this time, with an older state of mind. Recalling the experience with a new perspectives will be effective in letting you understand that the dark is not so scary after all. In the majority of memories, the assistance of a professional is needed particularly if you were deeply shocked by such an event.

3. Removing the worry.

People tend to be more afraid of the dark the more they keep away from it. In severe cases, immersing yourself in the very thing that you feared can help you redefine your idea of it. In the case of darkness, this means denying yourself of light to depend less on it for safety and security in the dark, specifically when you're sleeping.

Sometimes, you might have even had to re-associate darkness with less than threatening principles like safety, peace, convenience, and sleep. The hypnosis session will allow your brain to slowly get accustomed to abrupt lacks of light and help you respond properly should such emergencies develop.

You need not be haunted or incapacitated forever by the worry of darkness. Constant hypnosis sessions will help you realize that the dark is not as overbearing or threatening as you might believe it is.

Everyone in this world actually has a dark side - the Shadow in terms of Jungian psychology. This aspect of the self has the dark impulses, the upsetting inclinations within us. It is great to know this hidden part of the self.

So, here are signs if you truly know your dark side all right.

1. You are well aware of the method which your criticisms, judgments, and anger towards other people reflect your own weaknesses. The mental defense mechanism called forecast, especially colors how we come up with others. Sometimes we attribute to them qualities that are actually our own weaknesses.

2. You acknowledge that there is a discomfort, evil, and suffering on the planet. Recognizing the evil around us can help us comprehend that there is also an evil inside of us.

3. You know that often your words or actions can express fear and anxiety.

4. You know that often your words or actions can reveal enviousness and envy. Jealousy and envy are rooted in selfishness, a selfishness that is □uite hard to root out.

5. You know that there are times your words or actions reveal covetousness and greed. Covetousness and greed come from our attachment to the product and temporal things of this world.

6. You know that there are times your words reveal contempt and spite. Contempt and spite for other ones are born of anger and hatred - fruits of not being able to handle aggravation in a favorable manner.

7. You are well aware of your fears and anxieties.

8. You are actually aware of your feelings of enviousness and envy.

9. You are actually aware of your emotions of greed.

10. You are aware of your feelings of anger. Being aware of these types of feelings can make you understand certain actions (consisting of saying something) that you find involuntary. In some cases, we do not mean to injure people but deep inside, these emotions are still there, so unconsciously we do injure people. It is best to be aware of these negative emotions and then process them through psychotherapy.

Understanding your dark side makes it possible for and empowers you to start certain life-altering changes. Now you can know what ticks you off, and you can begin to change appropriately. You can steer more clearly from temptation and other allurements. Obviously, temptation doesn't vanish entirely, but you are no longer unprepared to handle certain circumstance.

BENEFITS OF A DARK SIDE

In psychology, an aspect of our own self is given the name of the Shadow (based upon Carl Jung's theories). This Shadow is our dark impulses, our "dark side" so to speak-a hidden part of our self that we typically do not want to show even to our own selves. We may not know this aspect-we might even be afraid to face it. But it is best to meet our dark side for the following benefits:

You can use your creativity and imagination to acknowledge the disowned part of your own self. Certain activities about exploring the Shadow focus on drawing, mind-mapping and so on. Making associations with our creative side can boost our connection to that concealed part inside all of us.

You can heal any relationship with regard to having more honest self-examination, and a direct sort of communication. Since certain relationships are harmed just because of concealed animosities, the more we see what we hide, the more we can understand those relationships that are simply broken or ended for no evident reason.

You can recognize what you "job" unto others, which then forms some of our viewpoints about other people. All of us tend to see in other ones what we anticipate from ourselves. So instead of really knowing the other, we are making "theories" on what the other is like based upon what we know from us.

Almost automatically, we might tend to think and ask, "What do I do if I were him or her?" This is really a pretty good ⬜uestion if one knows that he or she is asking it, and not using the believed to judge someone's actions or thoughts rashly.

You can start to be free of the guilt and the embarassment that features your negative feelings, and obviously, perhaps, bad actions. Certainly, we can see why there is a real psychological gain from the Catholic practice of confession. In all possible great ways, we really need to be confronted with our battle and our dark impulses to be devoid of them.

You can pacify whatever negative emotions that come as you set about your routine in your daily life. We really need to be reconciled with negative events and situations that disturb us suddenly.

Lastly, you can achieve authentic self-acceptance, a complete sort of self-knowledge-of who you are and who you can be.

Machiavellianism in psychology refers to a personality trait which sees a person so concentrated on their own interests they will control, deceive, and exploit others to achieve their goals.

Machiavellianism is one of the traits in what is called the 'Dark Triad', the other two being narcissism and psychopathy.

The term itself derives from a reference to the infamous Niccolò Machiavelli, a diplomat and theorist in the Renaissance whose most well-known work ended up being 'The Prince" (Il Principe). This infamous book embraced his views that strong rulers should be extreme with their subjects and enemies, and that magnificence and survival warranted any means, even ones that were considered unethical and brutal.

By the late 16th century "Machiavellianism" ended up being a well-known word to define the art of being deceptive to get ahead.

Just find a therapist

But it wasn't a psychological term until the 1970s, when 2 social psychologists, Richard Christie and Florence L. Geis, developed what they called "the Machiavellianism Scale". A personality inventory that is still used as the primary assessement tool for Machaivellianism, this scale is now called 'the Mach-IV test".

Machiavellianism has been found to be more typical in guys then ladies. It can, however, take place in anybody-- even kids.

Signs of Machiavellianism

Machiavellianism in psychologySomeone with the quality of Machiavellianism will tend to have a lot of the following tendencies:

only concentrated on their own aspiration and interests

prioritize money and power over relationships

discovered as captivating and positive

make use of and manipulate others to get ahead

lie and deceive when needed

usage of flattery a lot

not having in principles and values

can seem as if aloof or tough to actually learn more about

cynical of goodness and morality

efficient in causing others damage to attain their methods

low levels of empathy

typically keep away from dedication and psychological attachments

can be extremely patient because of determining nature

rarely reveal their true objectives

prone to casual sex encounters

can be good at reading social situations and others

lack of heat in social interactions

not always aware of the repercussions of their actions

may have a hard time to determine their own emotions

The Machiavellianism Scale

The Machiavellianism scale is a score of up to 100 arising from a test that consists of a series of questions. People who score above 60 are thought about 'high Machs' and those scoring right below 60, 'low Machs'.

High Machs are focused on their own wellbeing. They really believe that to get ahead, one should be misleading. They do not rely on human goodness and think depending on others is naive. Prioritizing power over love and connection, they do not really believe that humankind is by nature great.

A low Mach, on the other hand, tends to show empathy to other ones, and is sincere and trusting. They believe in human goodness and that if you abide by good morals you will succeed in life. Too low on the scale, though, can see people being submissive and too acceptable.

There is also a 'Kiddie Mach Test' for kids.

Associated psychological conditions to Machiavellianism

Machiavellianism in PsychologyMachiavellianism is considered part of the 'Dark Triad', being among three personality traits that also includes narcississm and sociopathy/ psychopathy. With each of these traits alone making somebody challenging to be around, all 3 happening in a single person can make for somebody that is quite dangerous to other individuals' mental wellness.

Regardless of relatively apparent connections between the three 'dark triad' characteristics and the prevalence of one quality typically accompanying the other 2, research has yet to be done to concretely prove a correlation.

Personality disorders where victims might have the quality of Machiavellianism consist of Antisocial personality disorder, and Egotistical personality disorder.

A recent study also found a high prevalence of depression in those with the Machiavellian characteristic.

What is the distinction between the three personality type of the dark triad?

All 3 characteristics have to do with attempting to get away with putting yourself first to get what you really want. But they each have a much different focus.

Machiavellianism is mostly about control for individual gain.

Narcissism is mostly about thinking you deserve appreciation and to be dealt with in a different way than others.

Sociopathy is mostly about being cold and insensitive to other ones' needs.

How is Machiavellianism treated?

The issue with malevolent personality traits like those found in the dark triad is that those who have such qualities are not likely to look for therapy or want to change. They usually only attend treatment if pushed to do so by members of the family or as they have committed a criminal offense and have been told to participate in therapy by court order.

machiavellianism in psychologyFor psychotherapy to be efficient, a client needs to be honest and enable a relying on relationship to form between themselves and their therapist. Machiavellianism is a quality whereby a person is usually unethical and doesn't trust other ones.

And yet with an experienced psychotherapist development can be made. A very good psychotherapist with experience of the traits of the Dark Triad will see each customer as a private and take into consideration their distinct history. This will include the conditioning they have experienced and their unique life circumstances. A qualified therapist can also determine and help treat other associated concerns the person has, like depression and stress and anxiety.

Cognitive behavior therapy is one type of therapy that is often recommended for those with malicious characteristic. It espouses that the way we think determines our behavior, so by identifying and replacing disordered thoughts and emotions we can then transform behavior.

How Do I Know If I Have the Machiavellian Quality?

While you can find your score on the Machiavellian Scale by trying the test online, self diagnosis is not advised. If you actually are concerned you have the quality a correct diagnosis with a mental health expert is suggested.

I Am Sure My Boss/ Ex/ Family Member Has the Machiavellianism Characteristic, So What Do I Do?

The issue then depends on the simple fact that those who do have the Machiavellian characteristic hardly ever will want to change or seek aid.

Naturally it's also simple to assume others have the characteristics of the 'dark triad' like Machiavellianism, and while a lot of do, it's best not to leap to conclusions.

If, however, you feel you are the victim of someone with the Machiavellian trait, what you CAN do is seek help and support for yourself.

It can be frustrating and trigger great psychological distress and damage to have such a person in your life, and their capacity to control may leave you doubting your own impulses or sensation co-dependently 'addicted' to having them in your life. A therapist can help you learn better self-care, and help you set limits or if possible liberate the person from your life for great.

Control or manipulation is the practice of using indirect strategies to control conduct, emotions, and relationships.

Many people participate in regular control. For example, telling an acquaintance you feel "fine" when you are actually depressed is, technically, a type of control as it controls your acquaintance's perceptions of and reactions to you.

Control can also have more sneaky repercussions, however, and it is often connected with psychological abuse, especially in intimate relationships. Most people view manipulation negatively, specifically when it damages the physical, psychological, or mental health of the person being controlled.

While people who control others often do so since they feel the need to manage their environment and surroundings, a desire that often originates from ingrained worry or anxiety, it is not a healthy behavior. Taking part in manipulation might prevent the manipulator from connecting with their genuine self, and being manipulated can cause a specific to experience a large range of ill effects.

PSYCHOLOGICAL HEALTH EFFECTS OF MANIPULATION

If unaddressed, manipulation can cause poor psychological health results for those who are manipulated. Persistent manipulation in close relationships may also be a sign emotional abuse is occurring, which in many cases, can have a comparable impact to trauma-- especially when the victim of control is made to feel guilty or embarrassed.

Victims of persistent control may:

Feel depressed

Develop anxiety

Develop unhealthy coping patterns

Constantly try to please the manipulative person

Lie about their feelings

Put another person's needs before their own

Find it challenging to trust others

Sometimes, control can be so prevalent that it triggers a victim to question their understanding of reality. The timeless film Gaslight showed one such story, in which lady's husband discreetly manipulated her till she no longer trusted her own understandings. For example, the spouse covertly rejected the gaslights and persuaded his spouse the dimming light was all in her head.

CONTROL AND MENTAL HEALTH

While the majority of people participate in manipulation from time to time, a chronic pattern of control can suggest a hidden mental health issue.

Manipulation is particularly common with personality disorder diagnoses just like borderline character (BPD) and egotistical character (NPD). For lots of with BPD, control might be a way of meeting their emotional needs or acquiring recognition, and it usually happens when the person with BPD feels insecure or abandoned. As many people with BPD have seen or experienced abuse, manipulation might have developed as a coping system to get needs met indirectly.

People with egotistical personality (NPD) may have different reasons for participating in manipulative behavior. As those with NPD might have difficulty forming close relationships, they might turn to control in order to "keep" their partner in the relationship. Attributes of egotistical control might include shaming, blaming, playing the "victim," control issues, and gaslighting.

Munchausen syndrome by proxy, throughout which a caregiver makes another person ill to get attention or love, is another condition that is defined by manipulative habits.

CONTROL IN RELATIONSHIPS

Long-term control can have serious results in close relationships, consisting of those between good friends, family members, and romantic partners. Manipulation can weaken the health of a relationship and result in poor psychological health of those in the relationship and even the dissolution of the relationship.

In a marriage or partnership, control can trigger one partner to feel bullied, separated, or worthless. Even in healthy relationships, one partner might inadvertently manipulate the other in order to keep away from conflict or even in an attempt to keep their partner from feeling burdened. Lots of people may even know they are being controlled in their relationship and choose to ignore or downplay it. Control in intimate relationships can take tons of forms, including exaggeration, guilt, gift-giving or selectively demonstrating affection, secret-keeping, and passive aggression.

Parents who manipulate their kids might set their children up for guilt, anxiety, anxiety, eating concerns, and other mental health conditions. One study also revealed that mother and father who routinely use manipulation techniques on their kids may increase the possibility their kids will also use manipulative conduct. Signs of control in the parent-child relationship might include making the child feel guilty, absence of responsibility from a moms and dad, downplaying a kid's achievements, and a need to be included with lots of elements of the child's life.

People might also feel controlled if they are part of a relationship that has ended up being harmful. In manipulative friendships, one person may be using the other to meet their own needs at the expense of their good friend's. A manipulative good friend might use guilt or browbeating to extract favors, like lending cash, or they might only reach out to that good friend when they need their own emotional needs met and might find excuses when their good friend requires in the relationship.

EXAMPLES OF MANIPULATIVE BEHAVIOR

Often, people might manipulate other ones automatically, without being completely familiar with what they're doing, while others might actively work on enhancing their control techniques. Some signs of control include:

Passive-aggressive conduct

Implicit dangers

Dishonesty

Withholding information

Separating an individual from loved ones

Gaslighting

Verbal abuse

The use of sex to attain objectives

As the motives behind control can vary from unconscious to destructive, it is necessary to determine the situations of the manipulation that is happening. While breaking things off might be vital in circumstance of abuse, a therapist may help others learn to deal with or challenge manipulative conduct from other ones.

HOW TO DEAL WITH MANIPULATIVE PEOPLE

When manipulation becomes hazardous, dealing with the conduct from others can be stressful. Adjustment in the workplace has been revealed to reduce performance, and manipulative conduct from loved ones can make reality seem questionable. If you feel you are being controlled in any sort of a relationship, it might be handy to:

Disengage. If somebody is trying to get a specific psychological reaction from you, choose not to give it to them. For example, if a manipulative friend is known to flatter you before asking for an overreaching favor, don't play along-- rather, reply politely and move the conversation along.

Be confident. Often, manipulation might consist of a single person's attempts to trigger another person to question their capabilities, intuition, or perhaps reality. If this happens, it might help to stick to your story; however, if this happens typically in a close relationship, it could be time to leave.

Address the situation. Call out the manipulative behavior as it's happening. Keeping the focus on how the other person's actions are affecting you instead of beginning with an accusatory statement may also help you reach a resolution while stressing that their manipulative techniques will not work on you.

Stay on-topic. When you point out a habits that makes you feel controlled, the other person may try to reduce the situation or muddle the situation by raising other issues as an interruption. Remember your bottom line and stick to that.

ADDRESSING CONTROL IN THERAPY

Treatment and therapy for manipulative behavior might depend mostly on what underlying issues are causing the conduct. If, for instance, the manipulation is being caused by an underlying psychological health problem, individual treatment may help that person understand why their behavior is unhealthy for themselves and those around them. A therapist may also be able to help the manipulative person learn skills for communicating with others while appreciating their limits and address underlying insecurities that may be contributing to the behavior.

Certain psychological health concerns just like borderline personality may trigger people to feel anxiety in relationships, triggering them to act manipulatively in order to feel safe. In these circumstances, a therapist may help the person address their mental health issue, which in turn can minimize their stress and anxiety and help them feel safe and secure in their relationships.

Chapter 6: Empathy

In which way are empathy and sympathy the exact same?

The terms empathy and sympathy are typically confused and with great reason. Both of the words handle the relationship an individual needs to the emotions and experiences of another person. So, let's check out the distinctions between these terms and in which way they are most typically used by people.

Both sympathy and empathy have roots in the Greek term páthos meaning "suffering, sensation."

What is sympathy?

Sympathy is the older of the 2 terms. It entered English in the mid-1500s with a very broad meaning of "arrangement or harmony in qualities between things or people." Ever since, the term has come to be used in a more specific way.

Nowadays, sympathy is mostly used to convey commiseration, pity, or emotions of sorrow for someone else who is experiencing misery. This sense is typically seen in the classification of welcoming cards identified "sympathy" that focus on messages of support and sorrow for other ones in a time of need. You feel bad for them ... but you do not know what it is like to be in their shoes.

Consider the examples below:

" I've always liked Saturn. But I also have some sympathy for Pluto since I heard it's been downgraded from a world, and I think it must stay a world. Once you have given something planetary status it's kind of mean to take it away."-- Jared Leto

" Pity may represent little bit more than the impersonal issue which triggers the mailing of a check, but true sympathy is the personal issue which demands the giving of one's soul."-- Martin Luther King Jr.

Why does the word "nice" rub us the very wrong way? Why don't people want to date the good guy? What's so wrong with good? Does not every mother wish you would meet a good guy?

Unlike sympathy, empathy has happened used in a more broad way than it was when it was first introduced; the term is now most often used to refer to the capability or ability to imagine oneself in the circumstances of another, experiencing the feelings, ideas, or viewpoints of that person.

Think about the following interesting examples:

" As you grow older you have more respect and empathy for your father and mother. Now I have a great relationship with both of them."-- Hugh Jackman

" I have always thought about functioning as more of an exercise in empathy, which is not to be puzzled with sympathy. You're attempting to enter a particular psychological reality or inspirational reality and try to determine what that has to do with so you can represent it." -Edward Norton

To sum all of it up ...

The differences between the most typically used significances of these two terms are:

sympathy is feeling empathy, sadness, or pity for the hardships that another person encounters empathy is putting yourself in the shoes of another, which is why actors or stars often discuss it.

When something awful happens to a friend or loved one, it can be difficult to know what to say.

That's why we often reach for one of these common responses:

" Everything happens for a factor."

" This too will pass."

" Just expression on the bright side ..."

" God has a plan."

" I know how you feel."

" He's in a much better spot now."

" This could be a true blessing in disguise."

" Something better is around the corner."

Although these declarations sound good in theory, they hardly ever do much to help the other person feel better. Instead, it usually reduces the other person's real pain and does little to get in touch with how she or he is feeling.

I do not actually believe we do this intentionally. We use these statements as they have been said to us in similar circumstance. We have become conditioned to actually believe that these cliché reactions are the best things to say when somebody is hurting-- even if they weren't helpful to us when we were in that exact same circumstances.

But even if you haven't lost a partner or detected with cancer, you can picture what it might be like if those things had happened to you. That's what empathy looks like-- getting in touch with the other person's strong pain and attempting to understand how he or she may be feeling.

How to Show Some Empathy

Once you put yourself in the other person's shoes, what do you say?

To be truthful, showing empathy is a lot more about action than it is about words. When a friend or loved one shares something tough with you, she is mostly looking for someone to listen.

But, if you are somebody who struggles with what to say in these situations, the following list might help you find a much better reaction than the ones we normally say.

Examples of Compassionate Responses.

1. Acknowledge their real pain.

Perhaps the best thing you can do is to acknowledge how the other person feels. When you get in touch with someone's pain or struggle, it helps him feel supported. It shows you comprehend (or are attempting to understand) how he might be feeling.

People in real pain really just want to be heard. They want recognition that what they are going through is challenging.

Here are some examples of what this seems like:

" I'm sorry you are going through this."

" Wow, that truly sucks."

" I dislike that this happened."

" That need to be tough."

" That sounds truly challenging."

" I can see how that would be challenging."

2. Share how you feel.

In some cases, it's all right to just admit you don't know what to say or that you're having a difficult time envisioning what it would be like to experience what the other person is going through.

Whatever you do, just ensure you do not reduce the other person's experience or make it all about you. Instead, concentrate on sharing your emotions to help you better connect with theirs.

Here are some examples of what this could sound like:

" Wow. I do not know what to say."

" I can't imagine what you need to be going through."

" I wish I could make it better."

" My heart hurts for you."

" It makes me really miserable to hear this took place."

3. Show gratitude that the person opened up.

Many individuals struggle with vulnerability as they have been burned right before. They don't want to share their struggles for fear that they will not receive an understanding reaction. I definitely felt that way for a very long time.

When somebody chooses to open the door to you, it shows they actually trust you. It's your job to honor that and respond with care.

Let the person know you really appreciate her sharing with you and acknowledge that it may have been tough to do so. When you do this, it signals that you are a safe port for vulnerability.

Here's what these reactions may seem like:

" Thank you for showing me."

" I'm glad you told me."

" Thank you for trusting me with this. That actually means a lot."

" This need to be hard to talk about. Thanks for opening to me."

4. Show interest.

Going through difficulties can be terribly isolating and lonesome. That's why people share their battles -- they are longing for connection. They want someone to take interest in their story and comprehend how they are feeling.

The best way to connect with someone is not by talking, but by listening. Show you care by asking questions and demonstrating an authentic interest in what they need to say.

Here's what that sounds like:

" How are you feeling about everything?"

" What has this been like for you?"

" I want to make certain I comprehend ..."

" What I'm hearing is that you are feeling _____. Is that right?"

" Is there anything else you want to share?"

5. Be motivating.

I believe many people actually want to be encouraging when a good friend or loved one is going through a difficult time.

The issue is that we often show this by trying to "fix" the problem or forcing the person to look on the bright side. And while our objectives are great, this method is rarely practical to the person in pain.

That does not mean you can't be motivating. You just have to bear in mind how you approach it.

Rather than saying, "it will get a lot better" or "here's what I would do," remind her that you love her. Share what you admire about her. Help her see what you do-- that she is a fantastic person who is worthy of love.

Here are some examples:

" You are brave/ strong/ talented."

" You matter."

" You are a warrior."

" I am in your corner."

" I really love you."

" I'm really proud of you."

6. Be encouraging.

When it comes to empathy, actions usually speak louder than words. You can show you care by giving a hug, sending flowers, writing a handwritten note or offering to trim the lawn or do the laundry.

When you do these things, it helps the other person feel loved and supported.

But, if you're trying to find something to say, here are some ways to articulate that you care:

" I'm here for you."

" How can I help you?"

" What do you need at this moment?"

" I enjoy to listen at any time."

" I would like to do ______ for you."

There is No Script for the Virtue of Empathy

The reality is that there is no script for empathy. It's less about what you say and more about appearing and listening well.

But, I hope that these examples help you stay away from the well-worn cliches and find a much better way to express empathy to those around you.

Showing Empathy at Work

Develop empathy to understand and help other ones.

Empathy is a lot like a universal solvent. Any problem immersed in empathy ends up being soluble.

-- Simon Baron-Cohen, British medical psychologist, and professor of developmental psychopathology, University of Cambridge.

Comprehending other people's feelings is an important skill in the office. It can allow us to fix disputes, to build more productive groups, and to enhance our relationships with co-workers, clients and customers.

But, while most of us are confident about learning new technical skills, we might feel ill-equipped to develop our interpersonal abilities. And many individuals are self-conscious about discussing their own emotions, never ever mind anybody else's!

In this part of the book, we explore what it truly means to show empathy. We'll look at how several easy actions can help us to produce more powerful connections, to build a culture of sincerity and openness, and to make a real difference to the psychological well-being, and efficiency, of our colleagues.

According to influential psychologist Daniel Goleman, empathy is one of the 5 crucial elements of psychological intelligence-- an important leadership skill. It develops through three stages: cognitive empathy, emotional empathy and compassionate empathy. We go over each phase in turn, right below.

Tip:

Learn how emotionally intelligent you are by taking our emotional intelligence quiz.

And Mind Tools Premium club members and Business users can listen to our special interview with Daniel Goleman.

Cognitive Empathy

Cognitive empathy is the ability to comprehend what another person may be thinking or feeling. It need not involve any emotional engagement by the observer.

Managers may find cognitive empathy helpful in comprehending how their group members are feeling, and for that reason what style of leadership would get the best from them today. Similarly, sales executives can use it to gauge the mood of a client, helping them to choose the most reliable tone for a discussion.

Cognitive empathy is a mainly reasonable, intellectual, and emotionally neutral ability. This means that some people use it for negative functions. For instance, those with a Machiavellian characteristic may use cognitive empathy to control people who are emotionally vulnerable.

Emotional Empathy

Psychological empathy is the capability to share the emotions of another person, and so to understand that person on a deeper level. It's in some cases called "affective empathy" since it affects or changes you. It's not just a matter of understanding how somebody feels, but of creating authentic rapport with them.

For some of us, this type of empathy can be frustrating. People with strong compassionate tendencies can become immersed in other individuals' problems or pain, sometimes harming their own psychological wellness. This is particularly real if they don't feel able to fix the situation.

You can keep away from this kind of psychological kindness burnout by taking breaks, checking your limits, and enhancing your capability to cope in such a requiring role.

Anybody leading a group will benefit from developing at least some emotional empathy. It helps to build trust between supervisors and group members, and to develop sincerity and openness. But empathy is most valuable when it's combined with action.

Caring Empathy

Thoughtful empathy is the most active form of empathy. It includes not only having issue for another person, and sharing their emotional real pain, but also taking practical steps to minimize it.

For instance, imagine that one of your group members is upset and angry as he or she provided an important presentation badly. Acknowledging their hurt is valuable, and verifying their reaction by showing indications of those emotions yourself even more so. But most importantly is putting aside a long time for them, and offering useful assistance or guidance on surviving the circumstances and getting ready for next time.

How to Develop Empathy at Work

You may have a hard time to show empathy at first-- you could be anxious about committing yourself emotionally, or feel not able to do so. But this does not mean that you're destined to flop!

To use empathy efficiently, you really need to put aside your own perspective and see things from the other person's perspectives. Then, you can acknowledge conduct that appears at first sight to be over psychological, persistent, or unreasonable as just a reaction based upon an individual's anticipation and experiences.

Practice the following techniques often so that they start to become second nature.

Give Your Full Attention

Listen carefully to what someone is attempting to tell you. Use your ears, eyes and "gut impulses" to comprehend the entire message that they're communicating.

Start with listening out for the key words and expressions that they use, particularly if they use them consistently. Then think about how in addition to what they're saying. What's their tone or body language telling you? Are they angry, embarrassed or terrified, for instance?

Take this a phase further by listening empathically. Avoid asking direct questions, arguing with what is being said, or contesting realities at this stage. And be versatile-- get ready for the conversation to change direction as the other person's thoughts and feelings also change.

Consider Other People's Viewpoints

You're very likely acquainted with the saying, "Before you slam someone, walk a mile in their shoes." Analyze your own attitude, and keep an open mind. Placing way too much emphasis on your own presumptions and beliefs doesn't leave much space for empathy!

Once you "see" why other ones believe what they really believe, you can acknowledge it. This doesn't mean you have to concur with it, but this is not the time for an argument. Instead, make certain to show respect and to keep listening.

When in doubt, welcome the person to define their position some more and ask how they believe they may solve the problem. Asking the right questions is most likely the simplest and most direct way to understand the other person.

Do something about it

There's nobody "right way" to demonstrate your compassionate empathy. It will depend upon the situation, the individual, and their dominant emotion at the time. Remember, empathy is not about what you really want, but what the other person wants and needs, so any action you take or suggest need to benefit them.

For instance, you might have a staff member who's unable to focus on their work because of a problem in the home. It may appear the kind thing to do to tell them they can work from home until the situation is dealt with, but work may in simple fact give them a welcome reprieve from thinking of something unpleasant. So inquire which approach they would prefer.

And remember that empathy is not just for crises! Seeing the world from a variety of viewpoints is a great skill-- and it's one that you can use all of the time, in any circumstances. And random acts of generosity brighten anybody's day.

For instance, you likely smile and take the trouble to bear in mind people's names: that's empathy in action. Giving people your full attention in conferences, being curious about their lives and interests, and offering positive feedback are all compassionate behaviors, too.

Practice these skills usually. When you take an interest in what other ones think, feel and experience, you'll develop a track record for being caring, trustworthy and friendly - and be a great property to your group and your organization.

Key Points

Empathy is the capability to acknowledge emotions and to share viewpoints with other individuals. It is among the 5 essential parts of emotional intelligence, and it helps to build trust and reinforce relationships.

There are 3 phases of empathy:

Cognitive empathy is understanding the emotion of another person.

Emotional empathy is engaging with and sharing those emotions.

Compassionate empathy includes taking action to support other individuals.

To use empathy efficiently, give your co-worker your full attention, watching out for verbal and nonverbal clues to help you completely comprehend their situation. Set aside your own presumptions, acknowledge your coworker's emotions, enable an emotional connection, then take positive action that will improve their well-being.

3 Empathy Examples To Help You Find Psychological Balance

When turning the pages of basically any newspaper, the world may seem like a bleak place with no empathy or empathy.

Nevertheless, take a much closer look and you are likely to find empathy examples in lots of places. It might seem like a cliché, but empathy can be as basic as providing an assisting hand to an elderly person.

It's an action set off by a genuine comprehension of another person's feelings. And fortunately, there are many empathy examples for you to observe-- you just need to know where to look.

What Are The 3 Kinds of Empathy?

Compassion is more complex than it might at first appear. There are actually 3 different kinds of empathy and each type features its own unique attributes:

1. Cognitive empathy

An empathic reaction usually begins with cognitive empathy It is the capability to sense how an individual feels and understand what she or he is thinking.

For example, cognitive empathy may give you an upper hand in the settlement because you know what the other party wants. It consists of reading between the lines and picking up non-verbal cues.

2. Affective empathy

Affective empathy is also called emotional empathy. It includes your ability to experience the emotions of other people. You feel the same strong pain, anxiety, or joy. This permits you to nurture a more powerful emotional connection with the people around you, but it can operate as a double-edged sword as it puts you through extreme psychological ups and downs.

3. Caring empathy.

This kind of empathy relocations you to act. Understanding and feeling what others feel activates the need to respond and supply help in any way you can.

Mindfulness is another essential aspect of empathy. Your attention needs to be concentrated on the exterior world. Use all your senses to pay more attention to your environments. Besides emotional understanding, it includes sounds, sights, and smells as well.

People who show empathy do not judge others. This may be much easier said than done, specifically when you meet someone for the first time. Nevertheless, remaining non-judgmental and impartial is an crucial step in ending up being more compassionate.

Try to put yourself in the other person's shoes to comprehend their point of view. In doing so, you should battle the desire to pass judgments and act on impulse.

Last but not least, don't wait to offer aid. It shows you want to dedicate your time to the needs of other ones. At this caring level of empathy, an empath might easily help other ones without regard to the personal cost.

What do you say for empathy?

Empathy is an exceptional tool that can help you build social skills and grow as a person. The ability to understand also makes it much easier for you to navigate complex social relationships.

What's more, empathy allows you to harness your emotional power to become more courageous and creative. It can also be used as a tool for widening your horizons.

Keep in mind: empathy means keeping an open heart and mind to others and getting as much as you give.

In essence, empathy isn't so much about what you say as it is about what you hear. Empathy is about being open and attentive to the ideas, emotions, and needs of others. It is the heart of truthful, real communication.

Conquering Self-Defeating Behavior

Have you ever found yourself pursuing an vital objective only to marvelously flop as you did something stupid?

Or, perhaps you feel stressed and restless when you're trying to attain something crucial. This, in turn, might make you feel increasingly more frustrated, discouraged and angry with yourself. These feelings trap you and keep you from doing what you need to do.

These are all indications of self-sabotage.

Self-sabotage deteriorates your self-esteem and self-esteem, and impacts your relationships with others. With every failed effort to do the thing you want, you "prove" to yourself that you can't or should not do it.

Recognize how to realign your thoughts, emotions and habits.

Whatever self-sabotaging habits you have, it's vital that you overcome them if you are to make the most of your life and your career.

Luckily, you can escape self-sabotaging conduct, and this text shows you how.

What Is Self-Sabotage?

Sabotage is the act of destroying or undermining something, usually in a hidden way. Usually, it implies direct and purposeful involvement on the part of the saboteur-- that's why the word is most frequently used in relation to spying, or in service circumstance where an expert is triggering the damage.

The term self-sabotage is used when this devastating behavior is directed at yourself. At first, you may not even see that you're doing it. But when negative practices consistently weaken your efforts, they can be thought about a form of mental self-harm.

Signs of Self-Sabotage

Self-sabotage can manifest in various behaviors, distinct to each person. But there are some common, recurring examples.

You may "forget" a deadline, or struggle to prepare a presentation effectively, for example. Maybe you're regularly late to work. You may postpone, consistently postponing something that you need to do, despite the fact that you know you need to finish it.

Perhaps you start projects but never finish them. You feel not able to proceed, even when you're presented with an exciting opportunity. Or you might dream of doing something of great personal relevance, but never ever get round to doing anything about it.

Another indicator of self-sabotage is that you grind to a stop for no logical reason when you're trying to accomplish your objectives. The ability and will are there, but something stops you moving forward.

Self-sabotage is usually driven by negative self-talk, where you tell yourself that you're insufficient, or not worthy of success. You find yourself thinking things like, "You can't do that!" "You don't be worthy of that." "If you try, you'll probably just struggle anyway."

We have likely all skilled behaviors like these eventually. But some of us are more vulnerable than other ones to self-sabotage, and it can be challenging to admit that we're doing it. So, do not overlook or undervalue the signs-- self-sabotage can reinforce a misplaced sense of worthlessness and supply a validation for negative ideas that have no basis in reality.

Self-Sabotage and Self-Esteem

One of the essential reasons people self-sabotage is an absence of self-esteem. This can have various causes, but the results are the exact same: feelings of worthlessness, the belief that you do not deserve success, and even self-hatred.

You may worry that if you flop, your family will think less of you, or that if you succeed, your co-workers will be jealous. These ingrained ideas and emotions trigger negative self-talk, which fuels your worries and your self-sabotaging behaviors.

Some people self-sabotage as it makes them feel in control of their circumstance. By undermining and then rescuing a situation, they might get a short-term increase to their confidence. It might even feel temporarily awesome. Nevertheless, these "rewards" turn out to be devastating in the long term.

How Self-Sabotage Will Damage You

Self-sabotage sets you approximately flop in a number of ways.

First, it strengthens negative habits that eat away at your potential for success. In this way, you might continuously find yourself disappointing the objectives you have set for yourself.

It can also harm your credibility. If you do not do what you say you're going to, there's a real threat that your boss and coworkers could pertain to see you as undependable, uncommitted, lazy, or lacking drive.

People who self-sabotage may also behave passive-aggressively, and have trouble handling anger. These tendencies damage relationships with good friends, family and colleagues.

Such failures and disappointments develop more emotions of regret and frustration. And, gradually, this can develop into embarassment, which feeds low self-confidence.

Defeating Self-Sabotage

1. Acknowledge Your Self-Sabotaging Habits

To stop self-sabotage, you first really need to recognize your own self-sabotaging behaviors.

Think of goals that you've had for a long time but have never achieved. Are there particular parts where you're postponing making a decision? Are you struggling with lack of inspiration, even for important things?

Consider something that you often fail at, for no apparent reason. Is there something you do, or don't do, that consistently irritates other individuals (your boss, in particular)? Is there an activity or job that nags at you and causes you discontentment as you know you could do it, or do it better?

It might hurt to ask yourself questions like these, but it is necessary. Tune in to issue circumstance so you can better understand what is going on.

2. Comprehend the Emotions That Lead to the Conduct

Self-sabotaging conduct usually originates from feelings of stress and anxiety, anger and insignificance.

For example, you might have deliberately left a report incomplete since your boss blanked you in the corridor, and this made you upset and upset. The event activated the emotion, which in turn led to a self-defeating action.

In simple fact, your boss might have been deep in thought of something else, and would be surprised and sorry to understand that they 'd upset you. But your psychological reaction doesn't take account of that.

Always aim to manage your feelings, so that you don't commit to habits that have negative effects, or that unjustly affect others. Check the cautionary signs of anger and stress and anxiety right before they get out of control.

Warning:

Make sure not to overlook strong emotions-- they're likely an indication that something is very wrong.

3. Identify the Thinking or Beliefs That Trigger the Emotion

Chances are, the feeling that led to your negative conduct was caused by illogical ideas. Think about the evidence for those thoughts-- in the example above, your boss wasn't being dismissive because they do not like you, they just had a ton of other things to think about.

Notice what you say to yourself when you participate in self-sabotaging behavior. Document all your negative self-talk, however silly or impractical it might seem.

The ideal time to do this is when you're participated in the behavior. Monitor your "stream of consciousness" and write it down. In our example, you might catch yourself thinking, "I'm such a failure, my boss has probably reached the end of their perseverance with me!"

When you know what your negative self-talk is, ask yourself what much deeper beliefs lie behind this self-sabotaging thinking. Are these beliefs rational? Are they based on any clear realities?

4. Change Your Habits, Emotions and Ideas

As you become mindful of the negative emotions, habits and ideas that set off self-sabotage, you can begin to challenge them. And if you can change among these 3 elements, the other two will change more easily, too.

Obstacle negative attitude with logical, positive affirmations. Turn your assumptions around and gain some much-needed perspectives.

Then, link this new positive self-talk to what you can accomplish and what you want to attain. When your abilities, beliefs and behaviors are aligned, you can produce the mental, emotional and physical states necessary to do whatever you set your mind to.

Caution:

Just changing your behavior is not likely to beat your self-sabotage routine in the long term, if you do not also change the emotions and thoughts that lie behind it. But it can help if you notice, learn from, and give yourself credit for more positive outcomes, as this helps to break the cycle of negativeness.

5. Develop Self-Supporting Behaviors

When you've determined and begun to defeat the incorrect reasoning for your self-sabotaging habits, you can begin to reconstruct your self-esteem. Think about the followng questions:

What can you actually say to yourself that is positive or encouraging?

What choices do you have? Is there more than one way to accomplish your goal?

Can you build confidence by setting and accomplishing littler goals, on your way to achieving the bigger ones?

Then use your answers to think of a message that influences you to move in a favorable direction. For instance, "Although I may not finish this project on time, I know that I have the resources and skills I need to get me through. When I begin to take on the job, I know I will launch a lot of the tension and anxiety I have been carrying around while I have been procrastinating."

Key Takeaways

Self-sabotage is behavior that undermines your success despite your own dreams, dreams or values.

The roots of self-sabotage often depend on low self-esteem, negative self-talk, and associated negative feelings, which are continually enhanced by the resulting failure.

You can beat self-sabotage by monitoring your habits, feelings, ideas, and beliefs about yourself, and challenging them when they stand between you and your objectives. Once you comprehend what is just behind self-sabotage, you can develop positive, self-supporting habits to keep you on the right track.

Why We Self-Sabotage

And what aspects trigger you to flip the switch.

We all have things we really want in our lives-- to lose those pesky 10 pounds, attain that big promotion, go on a second date with somebody we have an interest in, or take that fantasy trip. We set a goal that is near and dear to our hearts, and repeat it to ourselves in our heads and aloud to others more times than we can count. We have written this objective on Post-its, order of business, calendars, perhaps even thoroughly selected an image to put on a vision board, bathroom mirror, or fridge to motivate us.

We have shared this objective with our friends and family and announced that this is the year we are going to make it happen. Maybe we even asked one of them to hold us accountable to accomplish it. So why do we get in our own way? In order to comprehend where self-sabotage comes from, we really need to learn some key ideas about human conduct and raise our awareness of what might be running disturbance in the background.

You may be shocked to learn that the propensity to commit self-sabotage is built into our neurobiology and woven into the extremely fabric of what makes us human. In simple fact, its roots aren't so hideous after all. The source of self-sabotage becomes part of a common ancestral and evolutionary adaptation that has enabled us to stand firm as a species in the first place! To understand how self-sabotage is tied to our human presence, we really need to have a look at the 2 easy concepts that drive our survival: obtaining benefits and avoiding dangers.

We are basically set to strive for objectives because accomplishing them makes us feel good. That dopamine rush is a reward to repeat those behaviors. The technique, particularly when it concerns self-sabotage, is that our biochemistry doesn't necessarily discriminate between the kind of feel-good sensations we experience when we are going toward our goals and the "good" feelings we get when we avoid something that appears threatening. Apart from this, where animals stress only about physical survival, humans also have to maintain their mental wellness. In fact, an occasion that is psychologically threatening can activate comparable fight-or-flight responses as events that are physically threatening.

Attaining benefits and keeping away from threats are like 2 sides of a coin. They aren't independent systems, and there is a continuous interplay in the brain to try to bring the 2 drives to a balance. When we stabilize obtaining benefits and keeping away from risks, all is well; we feel good about ourselves, and we ensure our physical and mental well-being.

However, when these two desires are out of whack, we are primed to self-sabotage. Particularly, the pursuit of staying away from threats at the expense of achieving benefits takes us away from our preferred objectives. Self-sabotage occurs when your drive to reduce hazards is higher than your drive to get rewards.

So why do we in some cases overestimate a hazard and allow it to stop us from continuing on our course towards our objective? The answer is L.I.F.E. happens. In my research and through my experience in dealing with clients, I've found, time and again, that there are four components that sustain the conflict between going for what you want and being kept back by viewed dangers that actually will not damage you:

Low or Unsteady Self-Image

Internalized Beliefs

Fear of Change or the Unknown

Excessive Need for Control

These four impacts represent elements of your character and how you associate with the world. You can come up with them like an operating system that runs in the background and drives your beliefs and behavior. We generally obtain these L.I.F.E. elements when we are more youthful, and since they are with us with time, they tend to be beyond our awareness.

It is extremely useful to concentrate on them, so you can more easily see how they inform your choices, your ideas about yourself, how you behave, how you feel in certain situations, and particularly how they can be a motorist of self-sabotage. Learning to identify them will help you examine when L.I.F.E. is causing you to overstate a danger, and putting you on a course to self-sabotage. And knowledge is the initial step to stopping the patterns of behavior that hold you back from living the life you really want.

Why Do I Keep Doing What I Do not Want to Do?

Eliminating bad routines is extremely hard for a reason.

In spite of the fact that my father was a heavy smoker, and modeled for me how smoking resulted in ravaging health results, I became a smoker in my adulthood. Even though I know that he died of a heart attack when he was 58, and that this was in big part due to his smoking habit, I chose in my 20s to try it out-- I wanted to see what all the hubbub was about. While you 'd believe that my dad's emphysema and bronchitis, which made him wheeze just from walking to a much different room, would make me an intense opponent of smoking, still I stupidly picked up one cigarette after another and lit it up.

I can clearly keep in mind times when I was smoking and believing to myself, "This is truly dumb. [puff] I can't really believe I'm doing this. [breathe out] I don't even enjoy it. [cough] In the winter, I 'd have to leave parties and suppers to go outdoors in the freezing cold and look after my habit. I 'd be hugging myself tightly to shield myself from the cold, and bring my shivering hand approximately my mouth for another shot of heat and smoke. "Boy," I 'd be thinking. "It sure appears like they're having a good time there."

Why in the world did I do it? And why didn't I quit faster than I did? Reviewing it now, I comprehend that there is a behavioral reason that the practice continued, and that only a behavioral method to giving up could ever work. I wish to clarify how a routine like smoking can work against you, and then describe the types of behavioral modifications that I eventually used to quit for good.

Benefits and punishments: The foundation of every little thing we do

Once you're a pitiful cigarette smoker, routine in full flower, your body has concerned rely on the nicotine that you are ingesting at routine intervals. If you try to quit smoking suddenly, you'll find out that your practice is connected to really particular ecological cues that make your body anticipate the arrival of the nicotine. For me, these hints included alcohol, food, my marriage partner, my back deck, watching TV, and driving in my automobile. Simply put, everything.

Kidding aside, here's what was going on. Let's say I took a beer out of the refrigerator. I grab the bottle opener, and my brain says to my body, "Red alert! Red alert! He will have a cigarette!" My body, knowing that the nicotine and smoke are about to do some insane things like raise my heart rate and thicken my blood, gets ready for the nicotine and smoke by reducing my heart rate and thinning my blood. Why? So that, when the substances hit my system, they do not take me nearly as far toward a heart attack as they would without these changes. This is what psychologists call a conditioned compensatory response.

Each time you are in the presence of one of your cues, the body's attempts to adjust to the poisons you're about to introduce aren't that obvious - till you try to quit. Even if I cracked a beer and didn't light up, my body had learned to lower my heart rate and thin my blood. If I was no longer "fixing" the situation by smoking, my body's offsetting response left me feeling badly. This feeling was a penalty for not smoking. You catch that? I had messed myself up so much with my routine that my body was penalizing me for NOT smoking! And then, to make matters worse, if I gave in and smoked, the tension went away, and the positive sensation of the nicotine high filled my brain with a temporary delight. That positive feeling was a favorable support, and the bad feeling disappearing was a negative support, I was being rewarded with the positive sensation, and also with the cessation of an unfavorable feeling.

Before I was a smoker, these physical reactions to hints didn't exist. But once I was hooked, the ecological cues that were the antecedents to my behavior punished me if I resisted, and after that rewarded me twice over for being weak. No surprise breaking a practice is so hard!

I'll discuss a behavioral plan that can help you counteract your routines, and get you on the road to a healing. All of it starts with recognizing the nature of the rewards you are getting for your practice, and after that finding different (and incompatible) rewards you will give yourself as you quit. I'll break this down into small steps, so you can attain shorter and more frequent successes, and get the pleasure of getting progressively larger and more interesting benefits.

When Keeping away from Torment Causes Torment

Sometimes, you have to lean into your pain, not range from it.

There's a cruel, ironic twist to your efforts to avoid real pain-- you're causing yourself more misery in the long run.

It's something I see in my therapy office over and over again. Tons of the people who walk through my office door spend practically every waking minute of their days trying not to feel bad.

But their attempts to dodge discomfort introduce more misery into their lives.

A person who feels stressed reaches for his phone to mindlessly scroll through social networks. Although his digital device provides a short distraction from reality, taking a look at pictures of people who seem happier than he does actually contributes to his distress.

Another person feeds her loneliness with food. Sitting down with a plate filled with food is like salve on a wound-- at least for a minute. But as quickly as she's done eating, her isolation returns, and she raids the refrigerator again, even though she's not physically hungry.

These are vicious circles that are hard to recognize, not to mention break. But till you interrupt those patterns, you're going to stay stuck in a downward spiral of emotional chaos.

It's very likely that everybody have times when we look for immediate remedy for discomfort in exchange for longstanding real pain.

Here are 3 short-term options that might be creating bigger long-lasting issues in your life:

1. Numbing Yourself to Pain

Binge-watching Netflix and consuming a glass of wine (or two) to loosen up after a difficult day, eating as you're restless, and scrolling through social networks when you're lonely are just several ways you may be tempted to sidetrack yourself from your emotions.

Those strategies temporarily help you stay away from painful emotions-- and they typically become psychological crutches that help you make it all the way through bad days and difficult times. But suppressing emotions doesn't allow you to learn, grow, or recover from them.

In addition to your emotions never ever getting dealt with, those unhealthy routines can also take a toll on your physical health, social life, and mental wellness.

2. Keeping away from Hard Things

Stepping outside of your comfort zone is tough. Whether you take a new class or you make an application for a brand-new job, you're likely to experience stress and anxiety to some level.

You might make a mistake, humiliate yourself, or fall short of your objective. And that 'd be uncomfortable. So in an effort to stay away from that pain, it's tempting to play it safe.

Living inside your comfort zone is an effective way to dodge stress and anxiety-- but living a small life is also a recipe for depression.

3. Giving In to Instant Gratification

Whether you eat several additional cookies, or you can't withstand inspecting how many likes your newest post got on social media every couple of minutes, instant gratification comes in a lot of types.

And while giving into temptation will give you brief enjoyment, it will rob you of long-lasting joy. Plenty of research backs this up (including the well-known marshmallow test).

So while saving your cash, sticking to a much healthier diet plan, and staying focused on a job might appear like torture for several minutes, they are key to reaching your greatest potential.

Build Your Psychological Muscle

Managing your emotions in a healthy way is a crucial component of mental strength. And it's a two-way street-- the more strength you build, the much easier it becomes to manage your feelings. And the more you work on coping with emotions in a healthy way, the stronger you become.

Learning how to tolerate awkward emotions is an ability. And like all abilities, it takes practice. But as you acquire confidence in your capability to feel uncomfortable emotions, you'll discover that you're more capable and proficient than your brain gives you credit for.

Morality is readily evident that their account of what morality is happens to be a conscience-centric one, concentrating on self-regulatory behaviors (i.e. what you, personally, should do). These conscience-based accounts are exceptionally well-known among many individuals, academics and non-academics alike, maybe owing to its instinctive appeal: it certainly feels like we do not do certain things since they feel ethically really wrong, so understanding morality through conscience looks like the natural beginning point. With all due respect to the theorist set and the instincts of people everywhere, they seem to have started their analysis of morality on totally the really wrong foot.

Source:

This is the essential distinction, then: ethical conscience (regulating one's own behavior) doesn't appear to straightforwardly explain moral condemnation (controlling the behavior of others). Regardless of this, nearly every uttered moral rule or law involves punishing other ones for how they behave-- at least implicitly. While the specifics of what gets punished and how much penalty is warranted differ to some degree from individual to individual, the general form of ethical guidelines does not. Were I to say I do not wish to have homosexual sexual intercourse, I'm only expressing a preference, a bit like mentioning whether or not I would like my sandwich on white or wheat bread. Were I to say homosexuality is immoral, I'm expressing the idea that those who participate in the act ought to be condemned for doing so. By contrast, I would not be interested in penalizing people for making the 'really wrong' choice about bread, even if I think they could have made a much better choice.

While we cannot always learn much about moral condemnation via moral conscience, the reverse is not true: we can comprehend ethical conscience rather well through ethical condemnation. Offered that there are groups of people who will tend to penalize for you for doing something, this offers ample inspiration to stay away from taking part in that act, even if you otherwise highly desire to do so. Murder is a simple example here: there tend to be some benefits for eliminating specific conspecifics from one's world. Whether because those other ones cause costs on you or stop the acquisition of advantages, there is little question that murder might sometimes be adaptive. If, though, the potential target of your bloodthirsty intentions happens to have family and friends that would rather not see them dead, thank you very much, the potential costs those allies might cause need to be considered. Provided those expenses are substantially great, and certain actions are penalized with sufficient frequency over time, a system for representing those condemned habits and their prospective expenses-- so as to keep away from participating in them-- could easily progress.

Source:

There are 2 ways of responding to that question, neither of which is equally exclusive with the other. The first is that the cognitive systems which compute things like the probability of being found and estimate the likely punishment that will ensue are always working under conditions of uncertainty. Just because of the unpredictability, it is inevitable that the system will, on occasion, make mistakes: often one could escape without repercussions when behaving immorally, and one would be better off if they took those chances than if they did not. One also needs to think about the reverse error too, though: if you assess that you will not be caught or punished when you actually will, you would have been better off not behaving immorally. Offered the costs of punishment are adequately high (the loss of social allies, abandonment by sexual partners, the prospective loss of your life, etc), it might pay in some circumstance to still keep away from acting in morally undesirable ways even when you're almost positive you could get away with it (Delton et al, 2012). The point here is that it doesn't just matter if you're right or very wrong about whether you're likely to be penalized: the expenses to making each mistake need to be factored into the cognitive formula too, and those expenses are typically uneven.

The second way of approaching that question is to suggest that the conscience system is just one cognitive system among a lot of, and these systems don't always really need to agree with one another. That is, a conscience system might still represent a serve as morally inappropriate while other systems (those created to get certain advantages and evaluate expenses) may output an incompatible behavioral choice (i.e. cheating on your committed partner in spite of knowing that it is morally condemned to do so, as the potential benefits are viewed as being greater than the costs). To the level that these systems are independent, then, it is possible for each to hold opposing representations about what to do at the same time. Examples of this going on in other domains are not hard to find: the checkerboard illusion, for instance, enables us to hold both the likeness that A and B are different colors and that A and B are the exact same color in our mind at the same time. We really need not be of one mind about all such matters because our mind is not one thing.

Antisocial Personality Disorder

Antisocial personality disorder defines an ingrained pattern of conduct in which people consistently neglect and break the rights of others around them.

The disorder is best comprehended within the framework of the broader classification of character conditions. A character condition is a long-lasting pattern of personal experience and behavior that deviates visibly from the expectations of the person's culture, is pervasive and inflexible, has a start in adolescence or early the adult years, is stable over time, and leads to individual distress or disability.

The signs of antisocial personality disorder can differ in severity. The more egregious, harmful, or harmful behavior patterns are described as sociopathic or demented. There has been much debate regarding the difference between the two descriptions. Sociopathy is primarily defined as something significantly very wrong with one's conscience; psychopathy is characterized as a total lack of conscience regarding other ones. Some experts describe people with this constellation of symptoms as "stone cold" to the rights of other ones. Repercussions of the disorder can consist of jail time, drug abuse, and alcoholism.

People with this illness might seem lovely on the surface, but they are very likely to be irritable and aggressive as well as irresponsible. They might have many somatic problems and perhaps try suicide. Due to their manipulative propensities, it is hard to tell whether they are lying or telling the truth.

The diagnosis of antisocial personality disorder is not provided to individuals under the age of 18 but is given only if there is a history of some symptoms of conduct disorder before age 15. Antisocial personality disorder is much more typical in males than in females. The highest occurrence of antisocial personality disorder is found among males who abuse alcohol or drugs or who are in jails or other forensic settings.

If serial killers are some of the most psychopathic creatures in the world, is it possible for some serial killers to be more psychopathic than others? As it turns out, it sure is possible, and the killers on this list prove it. Sexual assault, burglary, cannibalism, and obviously, murder-- the following 10 guys are the most psychopathic serial killers of perpetuity.

Ted Bundy

You don't have to be American or have been around in the 1970s to know the name Ted Bundy. Bundy is easily among the most psychopathic serial killers (not to mention kidnappers, rapists, robbers, and necrophiles) of all time. His sick modus operandi included kidnapping his female victims, raping them, and them dismembering them. He often kept their heads as mementos. Before he was carried out in 1989, Bundy confessed to kidnapping and killing 30 women, though this number is likely much higher.

Andrei Chikatilo

Between 1978 and 1990, the Russian serial killer Andrei Chikatilo sexually assaulted, murdered, and mutilated more than 50 girls and kids. One of the youngest was nine years old. The psychopathic Chikatilo killed his victims by stabbing and slashing them with a knife. Chikatilo later confessed that he was only able to achieve orgasm by stabbing ladies, a fact that made it tough for him to resist his strong prompts to kill. Chikatilo was nicknamed the "Butcher of Rostov," the "Red Ripper," and the "Rostov Ripper." Though he confessed to a total of 56 ruthless murders, he was pursued 53, sentenced to death, and carried out by firing team in 1994.

Jeffrey Dahmer

No list of the most deranged serial killers would be complete without Jeffrey Dahmer. Dahmer, referred to as the Milwaukee Cannibal, was ultimately convicted of murdering 17 boys over a 14 year period. But Dahmer didn't just murder them. He also raped, dismembered, and often even ate his victims. During his trial, Dahmer confessed to drilling a hole into his victims' heads in an attempt to turn them into mindless sex servants. Although Dahmer certainly would have been carried out for his deranged criminal activities, he was beaten to death in jail in 1994.

Albert Fish

When a serial killer is dubbed "The Brooklyn Vampire," "The Moon Maniac," "The Werewolf of Wysteria," "The Gray Man," and "The Boogey Man," it's nearly certain he is thoroughly deranged. Fish was tried and found guilty of raping, killing, and cannibalizing three children in the early 1900s. Nevertheless, he claimed that he had murdered more like 100 kids, and even boasted that he "had kids in every state." Particularly psychopathic is the fact that Fish sent out a letter to the mother of one of his victims, 10-year old Grace Budd. The letter detailed how he had lured the little girl, strangled her, and then cut her in to pieces to eat throughout nine days.

John Wayne Gacy

There's psychopathic, and after that there's the type of psychopathic that defines the serial killer John Wayne Gacy. He was nicknamed "Killer Clown" just because of his job attending kids's birthday parties and charitable events as "Pogo the Clown." Gacy was founded guilty of raping, torturing, and killing 33 teenage boys over a six-year period. He would lure them to his home, kill them through either strangulation or asphyxiation, then bury them on his property. Gacy was performed in May 1994.

Jack the Ripper

Jack the Ripper might be a name that everybody understands, but nobody can be certain of his real identity. Whoever he (or she) really was, Jack the Ripper was absolutely psychopathic. In 1888, Jack terrorized the Whitechapel neighborhood of London by slitting the throats and abdomens of at least 5 hookers and leaving them for dead. Sometimes, he would even get rid of the lady's uterus and take it as a sort of reward. It's not likely Jack the Ripper's real identity will ever be figured out, but "ripperology"-- the research study and analysis of the murders-- has definitely influenced several "what if" books and movies.

Joachim Kroll

German serial killer Joachim Kroll killed at least 14 people, consisting of young children, between 1955 and 1976. After strangling his victims with his bare hands, Kroll would make love with their dead bodies, then cut them up in pieces to eat. Interestingly, Kroll was finally caught after a neighbor grumbled about a back up in the plumbing. The pipelines were obstructed with human guts. When Kroll was arrested, he was in the process of simmering body parts taken from his newest victim, 4-year old Marion Ketter.

Pedro López

Pedro López's deranged killing spree is frightening enough, but perhaps even more frightening is the fact that López's current whereabouts are unidentified! The Colombian claims to have raped and killed more than 300 women right across Colombia, Ecuador, and Peru. At least 100 of these were tribal ladies. In 1980, the "Beast of the Andes" was detained, and led police to the tombs of 53 victims between the ages of nine and twelve.

López was found guilty of murdering 110 girls in Ecuador. He also admitted to an extra 240 murders in Peru and Colombia, and was announced ridiculous. Exceptionally, López was released in 1998 for "good behavior," and while there are lots of rumors, nobody can verify exactly where he is today.

Gilles de Rais

Gilles de Rais was a wealthy knight and lord, a leader in the French army, and a companion-in-arms to Joan of Arc. He was also an absolutely psychopathic serial killer. Between 1432 and 1433, Gilles apparently sodomized and then murdered (or ordered the murder) of at least 40 children. Many naked bodies of young boys were found at his estate in 1437. A 1971 biography of de Rais defines the way the knight drew the boys to their deaths. He outfitted them in fancy clothes, offered them with a large meal and tons of red wine. Finally he confronted each boy with the "true nature of his circumstances."

Richard Ramirez

For more than a year during the 1980s, Richard Ramirez scared communities throughout Los Angeles. Nicknamed "Night Stalker," Ramirez would break into houses and brutally murder his victims, in some cases raping them first. His victims ranged from early 20s to a 79-year old female. His weapons of choice included handguns, knives, a tire iron, a machete, and even a hammer. Ramirez never expressed any remorse for his crimes. He was sentenced to death but died of lymphoma right before he could be executed.

No, you aren't crazy, you are truly onto something. This is what your gut feeling was trying to tell you all this time-- most of the time, an individual that tries to affect you to their own benefit falls under certain behavioral patterns. What that means is that they have several methods that they use over and over again to acquire the edge. If you know what you're trying to find, acknowledging and foiling their attempt to control you in one way or another ends up being a lot more much easier.'

" When you know what a guy wants, you know who he is and how to move him."-- George R.R. Martin in the Game of Thrones series.

A master manipulator makes you talk more about yourself than they do about themselves. The reason for this is that they want to find out about your strengths and weaknesses, to test your boundaries and even to cause a Freudian slip (a slip of the tongue). Yes, it may be genuine interest, but if the person you're speaking with avoids direct questions and changes the subject whenever you inquire an important question about themselves, you should most likely listen to your gut and not fall victim to their techniques.

How To Spot A ManipulatorYou are at work. You are really anxious as you have due dates and expectations to meet, numbers to crunch and a moving economy force you to be on the extremely leading of your game. One of your colleagues seems extremely interested, even concerned in what you are going through and what you need to say about it. After chatting for a few minutes you might think you have just met your friend in the whole world, but whenever it is this person's turn to speak about themselves, they rapidly change the subject back to you. Their questions are pointed, even purposeful and their entire focus is on you, even for minor subjects.

" Belief can be controlled. Only knowledge is dangerous."-- Frank Herbert

After getting to know you a bit, an individual that wants to influence you to their direct or indirect benefit might try to control the way you see them, e.g. they victimize themselves, they always put themselves in a valuable light and they try to condition you to respond in certain ways in which agree with to them. They might also try to twist the facts in a way that will lead you to respond (draw conclusions or take action) in a way that is favorable to them.

" Hey Mike. I am a little bit worried about you. Those jerks at the office are envious of your success and how that made the one in charge pay very close attention to your ideas. As a truth, the other day I heard Jennifer say something on the phone about 'that big-headed bastard'. I believe she may have been talking about you. This has also happened to me, I think we should have each other's back and point out to the huge man how important our ideas are. He'll know who to listen once he sees the apparent, no doubt about it." Observe how he reveals concern-- he is worried about me. He explains how he has also experienced this and unexpectedly the "I" ends up being "we" and his best interests become our benefits.

Intentionally or unconsciously, we try to drive our point across to our loved ones-- spouses, kids, good friends and even at work to impress our coworkers or managers. Purposefully or unconsciously, we find excuses for our conduct-- 'naturally I needed to tell her that-- it is the right thing for her to do, clearly' or "I needed another person that can translucent their actions and support my claims". Intentionally or unwittingly, it does make a big difference whether the manipulation procedure is a conscious one or not and if there is a well laid out plan behind it or not.

" And pity-- people who inspire it in you are actually extremely powerful people. To get someone else to look after you, to pity you-- that takes a ton of strength, smarts, manipulation. Really effective people."-- Deborah Caletti, The Secret Life of Prince Charming

So, what are some typical indications of a manipulator? Normally, they use several or all of these techniques:

They make you talk much more about yourself than they do about themselves.

It is the initial step in their process and they use it to discover your strengths, weaknesses, what you appreciate, what you abhor, what you fear and what you prefer with all your heart. Another word for it is reconnaissance.

They are trying to get you to be indebted to them.

My good friend's eyes will pop out of their orbits for telling you this (yes. I know, I'm giving complete strangers weapons to use against me), but this strategy deals with me typically. When somebody offers me generosity, I feel a responsibility to pay them back tenfold. It is not the case with Robert, but I have people knowingly use that against me. I am a big follower in the better nature of most of the people but I have learned through years of experimentation how to lower the amount of leverage that others have with me.

I have done that by ending up being more suspicious (a trait that I dislike in myself, but still need) and by offering brand-new acquaintances a small something, be it cash, ownerships or a small amount of influence to test them out. That way, the stakes are little enough that I will not hurt if I lose and can help me spot possible manipulators. Yes, you're right, it is virtually baiting and will not work if the other person is a master manipulator and waits on bigger jackpots. But it will help me escape the clutches of a lot of wannabe manipulators and, for the rest of them, I will let my newly cultivated suspicion foil their strategies.

They use small hazards to leverage their demands.

" If you are an approval addict, your behavior is as easy to manage as that of any other addict. All a manipulator need do is an easy two-step procedure: Give you what you long for, and after that threaten to take it away. Every drug dealer on the planet plays this game." Harriet B. Braiker

They manipulate the reality of the situation.

Master manipulators are also really persuasive and use their skills to change the way you see certain things.

They victimize themselves-- nobody comprehends them, but you might be the exception.

They suffer and you are the knight or dame (I needed to google the womanly equivalent for knight) on a white horse that concerns their prompt rescue.

They make you feel guilty, generally, by putting words you didn't say into your mouth or by making you feel responsible for things that aren't actually your duty.

There is a lot more to be written on this single manipulator technique and we will do it quickly. Until then, remember that you cannot save someone that does not actually want to be saved and you are not responsible for what other people do to themselves.

They continuously judge and criticize you.

They actively work at reducing your self-confidence. This has also happened to me a lot of times. It took a loooong time to get rid of the "I'm not good enough" and "No one wants me" beliefs. Do not let anyone tell you something like that. Especially friends, family, or significant your significant other.

They give you some false hope.

This is one of a master manipulator's worst offenses.

They lie with ease & if they are caught, they try to turn it into a joke.

Typically, their actions do not match what they say or assure. Lying comes naturally to them and, if you are a follower in the better nature of people, like me (they may call us gullible, but they are wrong), they'll have you caught in their web before you know it.

How You Might Unconsciously Help A Psychological Manipulator

If you have strong beliefs, safeguard them closely. Some of the best of us such as motivational speakers, missionaries, visionary leaders are really outspoken about their beliefs. But they also have some very outstanding track records and, with a remarkable amount of practice and some really strong beliefs they are the ones that influence millions, in a measurable, positive way. The beginning point for you and I is to measure our words and our really beliefs through the eyes of others. To do that, you really need to know your audience, their objectives and what it means for you if they choose to twist your words and use it against you.

Psychological ManipulatorBut, the words are just a part of your behavior. Let's put them aside and have a look at the other methods which you express yourself, just like:

your nonverbal communication

your intonation (what do you sound like if you only focus on the sound of your voice, not the words themselves).

your facial expressions.

your eyes.

your really presence in a certain place at a specific time.

You most likely have heard or read the following declarations numerous times: 'her eyes gave her away', 'he had a puzzled look on his face', 'she sounds afraid', 'he stood high', 'her presence encouraged me'. The method which you present yourself to the world is determined by your emotions-- your eyes never ever lie and your nonverbal communication tells a real story. If you do not knowingly secure these telltale indications closely, this is how psychological manipulators learn how to push your buttons, often without you even knowing it.

Searches just like "can emotional intelligence be taught" and "how mentally intelligent are you" have surged by 3-400%, according to Google Trends. This shows an increasing interest in finding ways how to interact better and more effectively.

If you will enable me, I will use part of Wikipedia's definition of psychological intelligence:

" Emotional intelligence (EI) is the ability of individuals to acknowledge their own, and other individuals' feelings, to discern between different emotions and identify them properly, to use psychological info to guide thinking and conduct, and to manage and/or change emotions to adapt environments or achieve one's goal(s)."

To make my point-- initial step is for you to recognize the emotions you might be feeling when you talk to someone else and to use that awareness to guide your actions and secure yourself from emotional manipulators by controlling your body language, tone of voice, etc. So you're probably thinking -- this is simpler said than done. You are definitely correct, I thought the exact very same thing while writing these words. Psychological intelligence and how to use it to secure yourself against emotional manipulators has a bit of a learning curve, but knowing your emotions and how they affect how you reveal yourself is an excellent primary step. Another way to prevent your body language from handing out way too much information is to set some well specified, particular objectives that help you manage your responses and accomplish what you really want. This takes us to our next subject:

" Why am I letting you comfort me?" He stared over her head. Since I have made certain you have no one else to turn to."-- Kresley Cole, Lothaire.

A master manipulator is different from the other puppet masters since she or he are excellent at what they do and also very subtle. They have 2 primary goals-- to achieve what they want and not be caught manipulating other individuals because, well, news of the sort spread quick. To achieve these 2 goals, they use their observations of other people to actively prepare each step needed to get what they really want.

There are roughly 150 searches each month just on Google asking these 2 interesting questions: how to be a manipulator and how to become a master manipulator. I did stumble upon a few people that behave like they have a Ph.D. in control ...

Keep away from contact with a master manipulator.

Yeah, I know, you're thinking "duh, are you apparent much?", but, if you can do it, keep away from emotional manipulators.

Say no to being controlled.

A lot of us pity others (that do not always deserve our pity) and accept things that break our better judgment. Just say no. The more frequently you practice it, the simpler it ends up being. You are still a pretty good person even if you say no every so often and you know this for a truth.

Neglect the would-be manipulator.

If you cannot avoid a master manipulator, then find ways to overlook them. Do not contradict them. Listen to them, nod and do whatever you believe it is best to do, anyhow.

Set personal limits.

Oh, this is so crucial, it has me quivering with impatience to put the words down on my computer system screen. Setting boundaries is ohhh, so crucial in any kind of relationship. It is a lot easier to do so at the very start of the relationship when people do not know what to expect of you, than it is to change course midway, when the will begin asking questions and try to make you feel guilty for doing it. How to do it? Let them know, plainly, that you will decline certain behavior: "No, I am sorry, you cannot use my notes, I put a ton of work into them and I wish to present them myself when I am done with the initial draft." It's sorta like the second point, saying no, but is saying no with a purpose. "No, I will not go with you to the one in charge to pitch in your half-assed idea and help you ask for a promotion."; "No, you cannot call me every night, we aren't in a relationship and I need to study for my exam." "I will call you when I have the time to do so." or "Stop calling please, you are a very good person, but we are not a good match. I think you're better off trying to find someone that matches more with you."

Set goals and you will notice if someone tries to control you from them.

If you plainly define your goals (individual improvement, professional career, health, financial and relationship goals) it will become that much harder for someone else to control you to their on benefit. When you know where you are going, your course on how to arrive ends up being a lot more clear and you'll have the ability to see diversions and detours from that course for what they actually are.

Assume duty for what you do.

Good or bad. Manipulators particularly at work, tend to make the most of other's people work and declare it for their own and they are actually good at blaming another person for their own errors.

Keep track of everything you are involved in.

Calls, text messages, conferences, your work, their work (whatever you have access to), finances, etc. Make certain you do not go too far and infringe on their right to personal privacy by recording, using keeping track of software application without their knowledge/consent because it can have serious legal consequences. Review office privacy and partner tracking before you do anything. It is normally acceptable for you to keep a note pad or a dairy with times and days and a description of what occurred. Make sure you leave a proof and/or files on your computer detailing your personal work and your individual part in a work project. Keep your call history part of the phone expense and save the text messages and e-mails you get.

Do not get emotionally included, your emotions can be controlled.

I am still working on this one myself, but I believe I'm making progress. Master manipulators will twist and blow your emotions out of percentage once they find out which buttons to push.

Acknowledge mental illness when you see it.

Often there is no manipulator to outsmart, but just an illness in need of treatment.

Be someone they 'd rather avoid messing with.

This goes together with setting boundaries. Make it too tough to get what they want from you and too risky for them to be found if they try to manipulate you.

Strike them where it hurts.

Turn their allies into enemies. Damage their power base. Let the other girls know he's unfaithful. Ensure what you do doesn't land you in more trouble than it resolves.

But wait, there's a 12th way on how to deal with a master manipulator (not recommended):

How To Control A Manipulator.

Manipulate A ManipulatorAs Athena Walker masterfully defines it in her answer on Quora:

" In regular transactions, the issue with outwitting is that it usually takes control to do this. We manipulate all of the time. It is how we live our lives. So, attempting to turn that around and applying it to me, chances are the tactic you are going to use, I have used it. I have used it, abused it, and already grown past it. So, I will acknowledge it quickly. [...]

It is tended to be recommended to not try it since we are great at studying you, whereas you are less likely to be as proficient at studying us."

If you, though, choose to go on with it, make certain the possibility of failure is acceptable to you. Be client. Be really subtle. Observe, learn and evaluate your conclusions, ever so subtly as to not disrupt their suspicions.

We asked catfish why they fool people on the internet-- it's not about money

Our possibility of falling victim to catfish frauds is increasing together with our screen time. Credit: Shutterstock

If you have engaged with web culture at all recently, you have probably encountered the term "catfish", first coined in the 2010 documentary of the exact same name.

A catfish is someone who uses incorrect info to cultivate a personality online that does not represent their real identity. This typically includes using taken or modified pictures, typically drawn from an unwitting third party.

Catfish will use this information to produce a more appealing version of themselves, then engage in continued one-on-one interactions with another person (or people) who are uninformed of the deceptiveness.

Falling prey to a catfish

In the 2010 documentary, Nev Schulman learns that lady with whom he has developed an online relationship over nine months is actually fake. Another wife (who initially said to be her mother) has used pictures from a design's account to create the complex, phoney relationship.

There have been some high-profile cases of catfishing reported in the media ever since.

Singer Casey Donovan, in her 2014 memoir, wrote about a six-year relationship that turned out to be fake-- in her case, the catfish even lied about her gender.

In 2011, NBA star Chris Andersen became involved in a catfishing scandal that ended in prison time for the catfish.

Then there is the well-known MTV reality docuseries, hosted by catfish victim Nev Schulman himself. It is presently in its seventh season of" [taking] online romances into the real world".

A complicated issue

Since 2016, the Australian Competition and Customer Commission (ACCC) has gathered and released information on dating and romance scams.

Its website offers in-depth data of reported romance fraud in Australia, yet there is little info available about social catfishing-- deceptiveness in the lack of monetary fraud. There are also questions about the legality of impersonating somebody who does not exist.

Till these problems are fixed, there is no clear opportunity to go after for victims of social catfish. Victims may stay uninformed of the deceptiveness for months or years-- another reason catfishing usually goes unreported-- making it even harder to measure.

The personality traits of catfish scammers

As smartphones and connected gadgets become ever more pervasive, the chances of falling victim to deception are increasing together with our screen time.

But what sort of person becomes a social catfish?

We have begun mental research to examine this question. In the past year we have hired 27 people from around the globe who self-identified as catfish for online interviews.

The interviews focused primarily on their inspirations and emotions about their catfishing behaviour. Some of our key findings included:

Isolation was mentioned by 41% of the participants as the reason for their catfishing. One participant said: "I just wanted to be more well-known and make good friends that could speak to me, some part of the day."

Others claimed that a lonely childhood and ongoing battles with social connection were contributing factors.

Dissatisfaction with their physical appearance was also a common theme, represented in around one-third of reactions: "I had tons of self-esteem problems ... I actually consider myself ugly and unappealing ... The only way I have had relationships has been online and with an incorrect identity. "

Another participant said: "If I try to send my real, unedited images to anybody that seems nice, they stop responding to me. It's a form of escapism, or a way of screening what life would be kind of like if you were the same person but more physically attractive."

Some reported using incorrect identities or personas to explore their sexuality or gender identity. For instance: "I was catfishing ladies since I am drawn in to women but have never acted upon it ... I pretend to be a guy as I would choose to be in the male role of a heterosexual relationship than a woman in a homosexual relationship."

More than two-thirds of reactions discussed a desire to leave: "It could appear magical, being able to escape your insecurities ... But in the end, it only aggravates them."

Many reported feelings of guilt and self-loathing around their misleading behaviour: "It's hard to stop the addiction. Reality hit, and I felt like a bad human."

More than one-third of participants expressed a desire to confess to their victims, and some had continued relations with them even after coming clean.

Somewhat remarkably, around a quarter of participants said they began catfishing out of practicality, or just because of some outside scenario. One said: "Being too young for a website or game meant I had to lie about my age to people, leading to building a complete personality."

No easy answer

What does it take to become a catfish, and how should we deal with this growing problem? Unsurprisingly, our preliminary research suggests that there's no simple answer.

Social catfishing appears to offer an outlet for the expression of various desires and advises. Although not yet formally a criminal activity, it is never ever a victimless act.

As we move farther online each year, the burden of hazardous online behaviour ends up being greater to society, and a better understanding of the concerns are needed if we are to reduce harm in the future. From our small study, it appears that catfish themselves aren't widely malicious.

Psychologist Jean Twenge has argued that the post-millenial generation is growing up with smartphones in hand at an early age and are hence investing more time in the reasonably "safe" online world than in real-life interactions, particularly compared to prior generations.

Catfishing will likely become a more common side-effect for this generation in particular.

The next phase of our research is to learn what we can do to help both victims and the catfish themselves. We intend to recruit at least 120 people who have catfished so that we can develop a more comprehensive picture of their personalities. If you have been a catfish, or know somebody who has, please call us to take part in our research.

Emotional blackmail is a dysfunctional form of control that people use to put demands and threaten victims to get what they really want. The undertone of emotional blackmail is if you don't do what I want when I really want it, you will suffer.

The Meaning of Psychological Blackmail

Emotional blackmail is the procedure in which an individual makes needs and risks to manipulative another person to get what they want. It is a kind of psychological abuse, triggering damage to the victims. Their demands are typically meant to control a victim's conduct through unhealthy ways.

Emotional blackmail is a way of being controlled by your partner. However, in these situations, it can be tough to determine and plainly indicate whether the victim is being controlled.

Leaders in the field, Susan Forward and Donna Frazier identify the power dynamic that occurs in such control. They suggest that emotional blackmailers employ a fear-- feeling-- regret technique to get what they want.

FOG is a term named by Forward, suggesting that worry, commitment, and regret are the characteristics in emotional blackmail between the manipulator and the victim. The acronym FOG also accurately describes the confusion and lack of clearness and thinking that can occur in these social characteristics. Emotional blackmail can create a fog and contribute to emotions of fear, obligation, regret, and stress and anxiety.

According to Forward, emotional blackmail takes place in close relationships. The manipulator leverages knowledge acquired about the victim's worries. Blackmailers will use the information they learn more about what the victim fears to manipulate them.

Forward suggests that one of the most painful aspects of emotional blackmail is that they use individual information about the victim's vulnerabilities against them. Another trigger a blackmailer will put to use, is putting the victim's sense of responsibility to the test. They will frequently produce undeserved regret and blame to associate their problems to the victim.

They make risks associated to the victim's psychological triggers to force compliance. For instance, "If you do not do what I want I will ... leave you, tell your secrets, not love you ..." They can also take advantage of the victim's sense of obligation and obligation. "All I do is work for this family, the least you could do is ..." Blackmailers make use of the victim's sense of regret to produce confusion and get the victim to succumb to their need.

As the techniques can be concealed, emotional blackmail may be challenging to find, particularly for those who may experience more weaknesses to it. According to Forward,

" Blackmailers make it almost impossible to see how they're manipulating us, as they set a thick fog that obscures their actions. All the while, if we attempt to fight back, they ensure that we literally can't see what is going on to us."

They can use concealed techniques that produce confusion by:

Making their needs appear reasonable

Make the victim feel self-centered

Pathologizing or making the victim seem as though they are insane

Ally with somebody of influence to intimidate the victim

There are cautioning signs of emotional blackmail in a relationship:

If someone regularly apologizes for things that are not their doing, like the manipulator's outburst, bad day, or negative behaviors.

If one person demands only their way or nothing, even if it is at the expense of the partner.

It seems to be a one-way street of sacrifice and compliance.

Someone feels daunted or threatened to obey or comply.

When in an inefficient cycle of emotional blackmail, the victim might be inclined to: ask forgiveness, plead, change strategies to meet the other ones' needs, cry, use reasoning, give up, or obstacle. Usually, they will find it tough to defend themselves, straight address the problem, set limits, and communicate with the blackmailer that the behavior is inappropriate. They do not consistently set clear limits suggesting what is acceptable for them.

Forward and Frazier recognize 4 kinds of blackmailing, each with varying manipulation methods.

Punishers-- Punishers operate with a need to get their way, despite the emotions or needs of the other person. Their slogan is "my way or the highway." Punishers will firmly insist upon pushing for control and getting what they want with threats to inflict damage or harm.

Self-punishers-- Individuals can make dangers of self-harm if the partner does not comply with what they want.

Sufferers -- this is the voice of a victim conveying regret on the partner if they do refrain from doing what is required. If they don't comply, there is an idea that their suffering will be the other ones' fault. "After all that I've done for you, you are going to let me suffer ...?"

Tantalizers-- This can be the most subtle and complicated form of control. There is a guarantee of what will be better if they comply. It sparks hope yet is still connecting a threat to the need.

Typical in any abuse cycles, it is important to understand the progression of emotional blackmail. It usually starts as subtle or implicit remarks and habits. The development can be sinister, so one does not understand its impact till it has gotten extreme.

A metaphor would be of the frog in boiling water. If you place a frog instantly into boiling water, its impulses will trigger it to jump out because of the instant pain. Nevertheless, if you place a frog in lukewarm water and slowly increase the heat, it doesn't recognize the real pain as a threat signal at the exact same level of heat. The frog ends up being desensitized as the water is heating up slowly. The habits and effect of emotional blackmail can be comparable.

There are six progressive steps recognized in emotional blackmail:

A need made from the manipulator. The manipulator will make a clear need of what they want, connected with a danger. You need to pay my rent or I'll leave you. You need to let me move in or I'll tell your sister what you said about her.

Resistance from the victim. After the demand is recognized, the victim may resist or feel the need to stay away from the person since they are uncertain how to manage the need. The concerning part of the process is it is often an unpleasant, unfavorable, or unreasonable need put on the victim.

Pressure from the manipulator. Manipulators of emotional blackmail aren't concerned about pushing too hard. They will persist to get what they want no matter what it takes. They disregard hurt emotions or fear being created. Creating worry can even be the driving force behind the need made. The manipulator might put pressure suggesting that the victim is being illogical, ridiculous, or unreasonable themselves. This part of the procedure can cause the victim to begin to question their sense of reality and if they are wrong in feeling concerned about the need being put upon them. They begin to lose their healthy sense of perspectives and what their gut is telling them. The manipulator may even turn the situation around to blame the victim or question their intentions if they do not at first consent to the placed need. Confusion is a huge part of this process.

Threatening the victim. This is the part of the procedure where the manipulator is threatening to do or not do something to trigger distress, discomfort, or real pain for the victim. If you do not do this ... then I will do this ... They create a situation where the victim can be accountable for the promised negative result if they do not comply.

Victim compliance. The victim gives up, either quickly, or slow through a process of increasing self-doubt. They abide by the need of the manipulator, usually triggering feelings of stress and anxiety, regret, worry, anger, or resentment.

The manipulator gets their way and subsides temporarily until the next demand of what they want turns up. The frequency of these habits and propensities vary in all relationships involving emotional blackmail. No matter the consistency of these behaviors, it has a negative and harmful impact on the relationship and on the victim. Now the cycle is in place and the foundation is set for this pattern to continue.

In some circumstance, there may appear to be a great line between indirect communication and manipulation. Emotional blackmail and indirect communication can both have passive aggressive undertones. The communication ends up being control and blackmail when it is used regularly to control another individual or coerce them into doing what the requestor needs. The victim will usually feel resistance to comply but does it at the expense of their own wellness.

There is also a difference between setting healthy boundaries and emotional blackmail. In setting limits, the person is asserting themselves and interacting what their needs are. Psychological blackmail includes conveying dangers that will result in a punishment of the victim doesn't meet the demand.

Someone taking part in emotional blackmail will demonstrate any or all of the following:

Telling you that you are crazy for questioning them

Controlling what you do

Ignoring your issues and pushback

Staying away from taking responsibility

Constantly positioning blame on other ones for their behaviors

Providing empty apologies

Using fear, commitment, risks, and regret to get their way

Unwilling to compromise

Seemingly unconcerned about your needs

Justifying their unreasonable habits and demands

Daunt you until you do what they want

Blame you for something that you didn't do so that you feel you have to make their love

Implicate you of doing something you didn't do

Threaten to harm either you or themselves

The Victim

Victims of emotional blackmail typically feel insecure, unvalued, and not worthy. They often struggle with low self-esteem and question their own needs. Victims can demonstrate the following attributes:

Approval looking for, people pleasing

Severe compassion and empathy

Propensity to take blame

Tendency to feel pity for other ones

Try to keep away from dispute

Peacekeeping practices

Strong sense of responsibility and doing the "right thing"

Worries of abandonment

Sensitivity, disposition to individualize things

Worry of anger

Insecurity, low self-confidence

The Impact

The tension of remaining in a relationship involving emotional blackmail can take a toll mentally and physically on the victim. It jeopardizes the victim's sense of integrity and self-esteem. It triggers victims to question their own sense of reality. It leads to negative and distorted thinking of themselves and their relationship. Victims of emotional blackmail typically end up being separated, experiencing extreme loneliness. It impacts a general sense of wellness and contributes to stress and anxiety and depression.

The Blackmailer

Forward keeps in mind in the book that an important takeaway for the victim is that the conduct of an emotional blackmailer feels like it is about you but for the most part it is not. It usually originates from deep insecurities inside of the blackmailer. Worry and anxiety can come out as rage and blame towards the victim. These tendencies often have to do with what has happened in the past rather than the reality of the existing situation.

There is no exact prototype of emotional blackmailers, yet they can demonstrate the following characteristics:

Egotistical tendencies

Self-indulgent

Extreme anger

Deep panic, fear, anxiety, or rage

Worry of desertion

Emotionally immature

Not in touch with feelings

Lack of responsibility

Dislike to lose

Some of these qualities might be close to the surface and observable, such as anger. However, much of the insecurities, emotional pain and worries lie deep within the psychological makeup of the blackmailer.

The scientific research on emotional blackmail, in particular, is limited. In one public health research study, scientists explored personality correlates of emotional blackmail in relationships (Mazur et. al).

They used the five-factor personality model to evaluate risk aspects for possible victims and people at danger for engaging in emotional blackmail. They found that neuroticism and agreeableness were threat factors for handling the role of the victim. The factors securing against using emotional blackmail in close relationships were agreeableness and conscientiousness.

Neuroticism is a key risk factor for taking on the wrongdoer of emotional blackmail. Social adaptation and assertiveness can act as protective factors against being a victim of emotional blackmail. Information was gathered to notify preventive programs developed to support people in building healthy relationships. There is room for extra research to be gathered and leveraged to aid with prevention of emotional abuse and blackmail.

15+ Examples of Emotional Blackmail

The emotional blackmailer typically doesn't have any other coping or go-to methods for how to communicate and connect in a healthy manner. They fall back to stonewalling, knocking doors, threatening, and engaging in other harmful habits to get what they really want. They usually do not have the tools readily available to comprehend how to convey their needs.

Lots of examples of emotional blackmail occur in romantic relationships. Any gender can take part in emotional blackmail. However, a male-female collaboration is a prototypical example.

One circumstance is if a guy in a committed relationship is caught cheating on his partner. Instead of taking ownership and excusing his actions, he might twist the story. He might blame his partner for not meeting his needs or being there when he needed her, therefore, apparently rationalizing or validating his conduct. This can be puzzling for the victim, as she may be inclined to question herself or begin thinking his claims. She may wonder if she is good enough or if she could have done more in the relationship.

Other examples of demands and threats in emotional blackmail:

If I ever see another man take a look at you I will kill him.

If you ever stop enjoying me I will kill myself.

I've already discussed this with our pastor/therapist/friends/ family and they concur that you are being unreasonable.

I'm taking this holiday-- with or without you.

How can you say you love me and still be friends with them?

You have destroyed my life and now you are attempting to stop me from spending money to take care of myself.

Emotional blackmailers frequently try to make the victim feel responsible for their (negative) actions.

It was your fault that I was late for work.

If you would not prepare in an unhealthy way, I wouldn't be overweight.

I would have gotten ahead in my profession if you had done more in the house.

Emotional blackmail may also happen in situations where a single person is an addict. They may threaten to take the car if the victim does not select them up from the bar.

Emotional blackmail can happen in family relationships as well. A needy mom may try to give her child a guilt trip for not investing enough time with her. She might make remarks referencing what "good daughters" do.

Emotional blackmail can take place in relationships. A friend might ask for cash and threaten to end the friendship if they do not comply.

A penalizing type of blackmail can occur. For example, if a couple is going through a hard divorce, the emotional blackmailer might threaten that if their partner files for divorce, they will keep the money or never let them see the kids. Such behavior can leave the victim feeling rage at the effort of being managed and not understanding how to properly react.

Another kind of emotional blackmail that is much more crafty is when we use fear, commitment, and guilt to hold ourselves captive. We can inflict our own FOG which can control our conduct, even if it is not originating from external sources. "If I were a really good child, I would visit my mom more regularly."

There can be different levels of emotional blackmail, varying from dangers with little consequence to dangers that can affect major life decisions or can be harmful.

Here are some extra quick and harmful examples of dangers connected with emotional blackmail:

If you don't look after me, I'll wind up being in the hospital/on the street/unable to work.

You'll never see your kids again.

I'll make you suffer.

You'll damage this family.

You're not my child anymore.

You'll be sorry.

I'm cutting you out of my will.

I'll get sick.

I can't make it without you.

How to Best Deal With Emotional Blackmail

If you or someone you know is experiencing emotional blackmail in a relationship, it is hard to know where to begin. In her book, Unnoticeable Chains: Getting Rid Of Coercive Control in Your Intimate Relationship, Lisa Aronson Fontes offers a "Controlling Relationship Assessment."

Taking an evaluation may be a advantageous way to begin showing and determining the violent habits that are happening. Her book also offers ways to help:

Acknowledge the controlling behaviors of all kinds.

Understand why this devastating pattern happens.

Figure out whether you are in danger and if your partner can change.

Secure yourself and your kids.

Find the assistance and resources you need.

Act to improve or end your relationship.

Regain your flexibility and self-reliance.

In Forward's book, there is a chapter called "It Takes 2." She encourages the victims of emotional blackmail to take real responsibility for their behavior and their prior compliance with the blackmail process.

The blackmail procedure does not work effectively without both parties actively taking part. Forward offers this perspectives not as a way for victims to beat themselves up or to place blame. Rather, she supplies this viewpoint as an empowering technique for victims to acknowledge what they can change and can control. In the intro, she specifies:

" Change is the scariest word in the English language. Nobody likes it, almost everyone is terrified of it, and the majority of people, including me, will be remarkably creative to stay away from it. Our actions may be making us miserable, but the idea of doing anything differently is worse. Yet if there's one thing I know with outright certainty, both personally and expertly, it is this: Absolutely nothing will change in our lives till we change our own behavior."

In order to best handle emotional blackmail, the victim must bring a new state of mind and technique the circumstances in a very different way. This will require getting insights into what is going on in the blackmail characteristics and learning to detach from their intense emotions.

It can be helpful for victims to explore what needs are making them feel uncomfortable. In doing so, they can acknowledge what limits really need to be put in place. They need to decide what is ok and not ok with them in a relationship. Understanding the violent impact of emotional blackmail is also crucial.

Valuing how emotional abuse is wearing victims down can confirm their experience of feeling hopeless and not having in confidence.

Change is frightening, but doing something different is the only way to get a different result. Otherwise, victims are at threat of letting their worries run and potentially ruin their lives. Awareness, insight, and educating ourselves is important, but change only originates from taking a course of different actions over an extended time period. Susan Forward asserts that all of us have choices about how to engage in a relationship:

We can accept things as they are.

We can negotiate for a much healthier relationship.

Or, we can finish the relationship.

No relationship is worth the cost of emotional and psychological wellness.

Victims can learn to set some limitations and may become surprised what can happen when brand-new limits are set. The messaging needs to become that the behavior is no longer acceptable. While victims do not feel courageous or confident after having been emotionally abused, they can take a different action. Victims need to do something about it to change the course, instead of waiting on the other person to change.

Victims can self assess throughout the procedure. When you do not back down and comply with needs connected with dangers, how do you feel? Strong, empowered, confident, hopeful, proud, ecstatic, brave, assertive, effective, capable? Breaking any behavioral pattern is challenging. Develop a clear vision of what you hope to achieve. Any change will need work, effort, and discomfort, yet this is where development takes place.

The only way to know if the limit and boundary setting will work is to try it. Forward suggests confronting the manipulator about the behaviors. What could that seem like?

You are pushing our relationship to the edge.

You are not taking me seriously when I tell you how unhappy I am.

We really need to find ways to deal with disputes that do not leave me feeling emotionally abused, worn out, and diminished.

I always comply-- not going to live like that any longer.

I really need to be treated with respect.

Let's discuss it, don't threaten and penalize me.

I'm not going to tolerate those behaviors anymore.

In her book, Forward suggests 3 workouts: an agreement, a power declaration, and a set of self-affirming expressions.

Contract

A contract notes certain guarantees you would make to yourself. The contract identifies the standard guideline for you to follow. Require time every day to check out the contract aloud.

Example of an Agreement with Myself:

I, _______________, acknowledge myself as an adult with alternatives and choices, and I commit myself to the procedure of actively getting emotional blackmail out of my relationships and out of my life. In order to reach that goal, I make the following guarantees:

I assure myself that I am no longer happy to let worry, obligation, and regret control my choices.

I guarantee myself that I will learn the techniques in this book and that I will put them into practice in my life.

I guarantee myself that if I regress, struggle, or fall into old patterns, I will not use slips as a reason to stop attempting. I recognize that failure is not failure if you use it as a way to learn.

I promise to take good care of myself during this process.

I assure that I will acknowledge myself for taking positive steps, no matter how little they are.

______________________ Signature

______________________ Date

Power Declaration

Another way to handle emotional blackmail is to create your own power statement. Repeating a power declaration can ground you when the pressure is shown up by the manipulator. For example, "I'm not doing this." "I won't do this." This power statement is concise and impactful. It works because it directly counters the belief that moves us into compliance-- that we can't stand the pressure. Short, impactful sentences like this are meant to challenge doubts and restricting beliefs.

If you start to believe "I can't stand it" ... that you can't stand to hurt his emotions, hurt him, deal with your guilt or stress and anxiety, and so on. Change the mantra from "I can't stand it" to "it's tough but I can do it." This includes a subtle shift to getting comfortable with being awkward. Changing to "I can stand it" will build your psychological strength so that you do not really need to instantly back down.

Self-affirming Phrases

By backing down and giving in, you might feel: guilt, hurt, shameful, ashamed, anxious, upset, weak, resentful, powerless, helpless, afraid, afraid, caught, dissatisfied, stuck. In order to change these feelings, it is very important to begin with changing your thoughts. Develop some self-affirming thought patterns to retrieve and repeat, especially when your negative thinking begins.

Think about asking yourself if a need is making you awkward. Why? What part of the demand is ok and what is not? Is the other person threatening me? Is the other person considering my feelings? If I comply, what is in it for me?

There are some levels of needs:

Not a big offer, minimal effect

Essential issues including your stability is at stake

A major problem involving crucial life choices and/or could be damaging

Demand that the blackmailer get psychological aid to learn new strategies. Blackmailers can learn abilities to learn how to negotiate, communicate, and own their own behavior. First, they must take real responsibility for their action for any change to take place. A hesitation to own and put it on the other person is a sign of immaturity and lack of health and wellbeing and health. Once blackmailers own the behavior, they can take the next steps to learn the methods.

If they are truly taking obligation, they will demonstrate the courage to take a seat with the victim and have a conversation about it. In doing so, this will create a more secure environment in the relationship. Safety is the primary component of defining a healthy or not healthy relationship. Manipulators who take accountability and want to be vulnerable show hope for learning and change.

What can that sound like in the blackmailer?

Can you help me?

Tell me how I can express this to you in a way that doesn't make you feel bad

I am willing to get assistance.

I don't really want my behaviors to make you feel so bad.

What is another way I can say this to you?

What can I do that will help you feel safe?

Where can I learn to better deal with conflict?

I want to improve how I communicate with you.

How to Stop Emotional Blackmail in Relationships

In a healthy working relationship, while stress and disputes take place, people learn to pursue a resolution. Emotional blackmailers are normally not thinking about negotiating. They tend to be black and white about their needs and unwilling to compromise.

Normally, they do rule out alternatives or other viewpoints. They really want what they need and nothing else. Many people who have been in a relationship with an emotional blackmailer really appreciate that there is no thinking when someone is in this state. The habits are illogical and the demands unreasonable.

How to stop emotional blackmail in relationships may start with the victim promoting the belief that they do not should have such treatment. Victims have as lots of rights as they do. As pointed out previously, acquiring insight into their own patterns of behaviors, pleasing, and approval seeking propensities can help understand where to make changes. The victim might have developed these tendencies early in life to self-sacrifice, overcompensate for other ones, and put themselves last.

Practical tips on what actions to take during an exchange with a blackmailer can be helpful.

Consider taking a long time out before you adhere to the request.

Take a break and think about how you are feeling about the demand.

Develop some distance from the feeling so you can make a healthy choice based upon logic, instead of the emotional default.

Put it on your timetable. It will create off balance and it can be frightening. There will be pressure to get back into the old patterns, so there is likely to be discomfort.

Forward suggests ideas just like repeating a neutral statement to the need put, such as "no thank you." This stops the back and forth and capitulation of the psychological exchange.

Don't really need to wait till you feel strong to show strength. Do it, then the emotions will catch up. People typically wait until they feel the nerve, and that time does not come. Do it, then you will feel better. You can't wait until you feel better.

Forward suggests extra methods to help stop emotional blackmail.

Establish an SOS before reacting to a need:

STOP-- I really need time to think of it.

OBSERVE-- one's own reactions, thoughts, feelings, sets off.

STRATEGIZE- analyze the demands and the prospective effect of complying. Consider what you really need and explore alternative choices.

Develop "powerful non-defensive communication." Sharon Ellison (2002) offers handy assistance on non-defensive communication. Recommendations are to not take the bait from the blackmailer, yet remain on point with what your key message is. Do not enable yourself to be derailed by their comments, demands, and behaviors. Stick to "This is who I am and what I really want."

Blackmailers are highly protective and their remarks usually escalate disputes. Attempt to stay away from intensifying declarations and stick with non-defensive communication just like:

I can see that you are upset.

I comprehend you are frustrated.

I'm sorry you're angry.

I can comprehend how you may see it that way.

Let's discuss it when you feel calmer.

It is vital to reinforce that victims cannot change their partner only their reaction. The emotional blackmailer has a foundation in deep layers of their insecurities. The victim's job is to put their well-being and health first. Their energy is best utilized to change themselves and their technique. In addition to changing the behavior patterns throughout these exchanges, victims can do their own mental healing outside the relationship.

For instance, developing skills to self-regulate, build confidence, and increase assertiveness can be beneficial. Victims can explore the following ideas:

Learn to become a separated observer. Healthy detachment is a great coping mechanism when handling conflict or highly charged emotional circumstance. It includes taking a step back and ending up being an observer of what is going on the existing situation, without being eliminated by the feelings at hand. This will allow some self-refraction and questioning to make practical connections between your beliefs, habits, and actions.

Creating some space between you and the situation can enable you to make healthier choices.

Forward recognizes the need to let go of pleasing habits. People who tend to comply, may give in since they do not really want the other person to be mad at them. They really need to rid themselves of the undeserved guilt, which is what occurs in emotional blackmail.

Expand techniques to handle your own psychological pain. Find ways to deal with your fear, guilt, and sense of obligation. Embrace the discomfort of the guilt, worry, or stress and anxiety that can come with saying no or developing a brand-new limit.

Continue to develop the thought stopping strategies to detach from worry and commitment. Obstacle your presumptions of what commitments and expectations are real and what proof is provided for these claims.

Review what part you play in the inefficient cycle of emotional blackmail. In order to be completely empowered and able to make a modification, it is necessary to look at your own obligation in the situation. This is not suggesting that you are to blame for the conduct of the other person; rather, to find regions and habits that you can manage to help yourself browse through such scenarios.

Take inventory. Self-reflect on how you might justify your compliance. Here are some examples of negative self-talk that can strengthen the pattern of giving in.

It's not worth it to deal with his/her anger

His/her needs matter more than mine

It's no huge deal to give in

What I want isn't important enough

I'll just do it to get him/her to calm down

I would rather give in than hurt his/her feelings

I am scary if I say no

Practice stopping briefly right before giving into needs in lower stakes situations. Practice saying no even when the risks are not apparent. Be firm and stand your ground on limitations set. Do not immediately give in to what the blackmailer wants, specifically if you are being threatened.

Seek expert aid through counseling, therapy, training, or a support system to help navigate through healing from psychological abuse. In the end, it is critical for victims to remember that abuse is not their fault. All people should have to be treated with respect.

EB After a Separation

A separation or relationship separation can fuel the fire for emotional blackmailers. The potential for them to act out, even more, rises up during dilemma situations, especially including a split. Throughout this time, victims could be at danger or at risk, as blackmailers can intensify their habits. Since they are focused on what they really want when they want it, they show restricted issue or empathy for the real pain of other ones. They can become so soaked up in their own rage, that they could show signs of panic in their desperation.

If emotional blackmail was used during the relationship and there is a split, there is no longer a direct technique for such control techniques. This can trigger a mentally unsteady person to act out much more if their ways for control are eliminated. Manipulator's habits may increase in strength and in a frequency. More severe dangers of self-harm and causing regret would be common in a separation situation.

They also might turn to stalking or other kinds of unwanted behaviors in pursuit in an effort to reconnect the relationship. While uncommon, brought to a severe, the ex might show compulsive tendencies and could be at danger for bringing the violence to another level.

It is important for the victim to bear in mind that they aren't responsible for their ex's needs and emotions. It is important to seek defense if the victim is feeling risky. This might need getting expert assistance to understand how to establish these healthy boundaries. It may include setting clear physical boundaries to guarantee there is no contact with the ex-partner.

Finding a support group can be helpful for people who have been in relationships including emotional blackmail and abuse. The focus post-break-up is finest placed on victims learning how to participate in self-care and identify their own individual needs.

Is It a Criminal Act?

Is emotional blackmail a criminal offense

In the legal system, domestic violence has been determined as an incident or series of occurrences including physical violence performed by a partner or ex-partner.

However, the laws dealing with emotional abuse are less clear and less constant. In the legal system, the term used to describe emotional abuse and blackmail is "coercive control."

The term 'coercive control' was developed by Evan Stark to help understand the effect and damage that takes place from psychological abuse. He determines coercive control as a pattern of conduct which seeks to eliminate the victim's liberty or liberty, to remove away their sense of self and is an offense of human rights. Emotional blackmail is a kind of coercive control used usually in intimate relationships.

Laws about coercive control (i.e. emotional blackmail) and abuse differ around the world. Presently, the United States doesn't have clear criminal laws in spot to safeguard victims from emotional or psychological abuse by a partner. There are criminal statutes that only safeguard partners from physical violence. Some states have attempted to house psychological abuse under statutes prohibiting domestic violence, child abuse, and elder abuse.

There are several nations who are attending to mental abuse in the court systems. The first country to ban "psychological violence within a marital relationship" was France in 2010.

Coercive control has been acknowledged as a criminal activity in the UK since 2015. The Serious Crime Act 2015 recognizes that "controlling or coercive" behavior towards another person in an intimate or family relationship is punishable for a jail term. Considering that the law has been in place, an approximated 100 men have been founded guilty and sentenced for such criminal offenses.

In the UK, for example, the law states:

Coercive control is specified by a pattern of behavior that slowly is purposeful in exerting power and control over another intimate partner. The law sees the perpetrator as the one who performs these coercive behaviors as entirely responsible. Coercive behaviors can include:

Making a person dependent by separating them

Exploiting their strengths and resources

Humiliating and putting them down

Using intimidation, or abuses that cause damage, are punitive and intended to scare

The British law specifies managing conduct as "making an individual subordinate and/or dependent by isolating them from sources of assistance, exploiting their resources and capabilities for personal gain, depriving them of the methods needed for self-reliance, resistance, and escape, and controlling their daily lives."

The law needs charges to be based on a pattern of behaviors rather than one occurence. Irish legislation have also created the Domestic Violence Expense 2017, that includes "coercive control" as an offense. In these nations pointed out, establishing criminal laws resolving psychological abuse sends a strong cultural message that it will not be tolerated. It conveys a level of support and security for victims of such abuse.

Domestic violence victims typically specify that the physical abuse was not the worst part of their abuse. The control, intimidation, and emotional blackmail usually caused one of the most suffering; yet the impact is more challenging to gauge. Author of Coercive Control: How Guys Trap Women in Personal Life, Evan Stark discusses the damage of psychological abuse and coercive control on victims. He states, "Not only is coercive control the most typical framework in which [women] are mistreated, it is also the most dangerous."

Identifying physical abuse is more simple, so the topic of how to prove coercive control or psychological abuse has been a subject of discussion. Those opposed to criminalizing coercive control suggest the location is unclear and tough to prove. Opposers claim that separating envy, control, and psychological abuse is complex to sort out and tough to prove by jury or judge.

Attention had not been drawn to the problem until the effect of the abuser's behavior on the mental and physical health on the victims was studied and assessed more seriously. More awareness is adding to more assistance and movement in the criminal courts. For instance, Monckton-Smith has developed a diagnostic tool (Domestic Abuse Recommendation Tool) to help recognize and clarify if victims are in threat.

Laws resolving domestic violence in the US were at first created for a very different reason. They were at first put in spot to deal with single violent attacks performed by complete strangers. Nevertheless, much of physical and psychological abuse happens in intimate relationships. For that reason, this law doesn't adequately address the cycle and pattern of abuse that happens with partners.

Critics show concern for the absence of assistance the US legal system is demonstrating for victims of such abuse. Without laws in spot criminalizing psychological and coercive patterns of abuse, the culture might be enhancing it. In his book, Stark suggests that in spite of its progress, the domestic revolution is stalled. He discusses how the narrow concentrate on physical violence against women, sidetracks from the more sneaky form of psychological abuse which more carefully looks like kidnapping or slavery than assault.

Stark considers the absence of laws dealing with coercive control represents a human rights infraction and a "liberty crime" against the victim.

The Center for Disease Control performed a research study in 2010, reporting that nearly half of all ladies in the U.S. (48.4 percent) have experienced at least one form of mental aggressiveness by an intimate partner in their lives. They experienced coercive control, verbal aggression and mad gestures in their partners that were degrading, insulting, dangerous, or humiliating.

There are companies and groups promoting for policy change in the United States. Their goals are for the US legal system to acknowledge the damage of coercive control and put criminal controls in place to resolve it.

There are alternative paths to take in the legal system beyond criminal statutes. Sometimes of emotional abuse, civil suits can be submitted. Victims or families of victims can file these emotional abuse claims based on an intentional infliction of psychological distress.

According to the legal system, Deliberate Infliction of Emotional Distress includes the following:

Intentional infliction of emotional distress is a deliberate tort based on conduct so horrible that it triggers the victim extreme psychological injury. Psychological distress claims are challenging to prove and win, and do not apply to simple disrespect or typically offending behavior. Instead, these cases develop when conduct is so remiss that the emotional impacts are real, lasting, and damaging.

In order to have an effective claim for deliberate infliction of emotional distress, a person must prove three elements:

Severe or Outrageous Conduct: Again, this is conduct that is more than merely destructive, hazardous, or offensive-- the conduct must exceed all possible bounds of decency;

The Conduct Was Intentional or Negligent: Negligent or irresponsible conduct will not suffice-- the star must plan to cause psychological distress or know that emotional distress is likely to take place; and

The Conduct Caused Severe Emotional Distress: This can be the hardest to prove, but serious and lasting psychological impacts like persistent stress and anxiety and fear, or possible bodily harm like ulcers or headaches could show an individual suffered severe psychological distress as a result of the conduct.

Tips for Caretakers

Emotional blackmail can also be used in families, even with kids or teens blackmailing their parents. Nevertheless, it would be simple to assume that all tantrum by children sound like emotional blackmail.

A kid having a crying fit at the grocery store because they really want candy is plainly a much different vibrant than emotional blackmail used in an adult relationship. Children may naively demonstrate such habits, without the grasp of the manipulation component. That being said, a teen making a need for parents to give them the car or they will hurt themselves does qualify as emotional blackmail.

All mom and dad are purchased desiring their kids to be happy. This potentially makes them more susceptible to being mentally blackmailed by their children and adolescents. Psychological health experts declare that this kind of control tactics can be very hard to identify and attend to. If they succumb to such manipulation techniques, father and mother can often end up sensation pirated by their own family.

Kids and teens can exploit your dream of desiring them to be happy in order to get what they want. This hijack can be resolved if father and mother are clear and understanding that the primary role is not to ensure their kids are very happy, but to keep them safe and teach them about the world.

Moms and dads that are handling a kid who participates in emotional blackmail can feel as though they are being imprisoned. Attending to these habits as a moms and dad is complicated and challenging. There is a range of seriousness in terms of the level of emotional blackmail kids can use with their mother and father. A common example might be a temper tantrum in the grocery store, where the parent, in an effort to stay away from a scene and to leave the store will give in.

Once mom and dad succumb to this conduct, the cycle becomes strengthened. The child then learns what buttons to push so as to get what they really want. They now know what to do so as to get the parent to give up. As kids grow older, the conduct may shift into disrespectful attitudes and remarks as a teen to try and manage the father and mother.

Teenagers can learn techniques to manipulate their mother and father by expressing strong emotions. In his book Declare Yourself, John Narciso identifies these conduct patterns as "get my way strategies." Teenagers, like grownups, can identify triggers for their mother and father and use this knowledge to get what they really want. An example of a button to push, is if the moms and dad is sensitive to rejection.

Teens can detect that and act in ways in which stimulate worry in the moms and dad that the teenager does not like them. This can create regret and fear in the parent, who then winds up complying to the teenagers' needs.

Another example is if a moms and dad is sensitive to inadequacy, the teen can slam the parent by attacking their proficiency. A parent sensitive to this might give in just because of the pain they experience feeling judged. If parents are sensitive to guilt, teens can highlight their emotional suffering to get what they want.

To re-direct emotional blackmail, parents really need to stand firm and constant with their limits, no matter the emotional outbursts or risks from the teenager. It is very important to clarify that acting upset or strongly will not change the mother's and father's mind. The key is to not be sensitive to these habits to the point that it changes your parental choices.

Some families, specifically those handling mental disorder in the family, will experience more severe forms of emotional blackmail. It creates a conundrum, as for children who participate in extreme emotional blackmail, common kinds of influence, discipline, penalty, or supports are not effective in changing the behaviors. A severe form of manipulation may include kids threatening their father and mother that if they do not get what they really want, they will tell people that they are being abused.

Here are some extra examples of kids blackmailing parents. They can blame their mom and dad for habits just like stealing, suggesting that it was not their fault that they needed to take the cash. The may say that if the mother and father provided them a larger allowance, they would not require to steal the money for what they wanted at the time.

Another example is that they make dangers to physically damage another brother or sister if the mother and father do not let them go out or do what they really want. They might threaten to escape if they do not get their way. Making a danger to damage themselves is another serious example of emotional blackmail. In these situations, father and mother need psychological support and assistance on how to finest browse in a way that will keep everyone safe.

Let's talk about Neuro-linguistic programming (NLP), which is is a mental method that includes studying strategies used by effective people and using them to reach a personal goal. It relates thoughts, language, and patterns of behavior learned through experience to particular results.

Supporters of NLP presume all human action is positive. Therefore, if a plan fails or the unforeseen happens, the experience is neither great nor bad-- it simply presents more useful information.

HISTORY OF NEURO-LINGUISTIC PROGRAMMING.

Neuro-linguistic programming was developed in the 1970s at the University of California, Santa Cruz. Its main creators are John Mill, a linguist, and Richard Bandler, a details researcher and mathematician. Judith DeLozier and Leslie Cameron-Bandler also contributed considerably to the field, as did David Gordon and Robert Dilts.

Mill and Bandler's first book on NLP, Structure of Magic: A Book about Language of Treatment, was released in 1975. In this publication, they tried to highlight certain patterns of communication that set communicators thought about to be exceptional apart from other ones. Much of the book was based upon the work of Virginia Satir, Fritz Perls, and Milton Erickson. It also integrated strategies and theories from other distinguished psychological health specialists and scientists like Noam Chomsky, Gregory Bateson, Carlos Castaneda, and Alfred Korzybski. The outcome of Grinder and Bandler's work was the development of the NLP meta model, a strategy they actually believed could recognize language patterns that reflected fundamental cognitive processes.This page includes at least one affiliate link for the Amazon Services LLC Associates Program, which means GoodTherapy.org gets financial compensation if you purchase using an Amazon link.

Interest in NLP grew in the late 1970s, after Bandler and Mill began marketing the method as a tool for people to learn how other ones accomplish success. Today, NLP is used in a wide array of fields, including counseling, medicine, law, business, the performing arts, sports, the army, and education.

HOW NEURO-LINGUISTIC PROGRAMMING WORKS

Modeling, action, and effective communication are crucial elements of neuro-linguistic programming. The belief is that if an individual can understand how another person accomplishes a task, the procedure might be copied and communicated to other ones so they too can accomplish the task.

Supporters of neuro-linguistic programming propose that everybody has a personal map of reality. Those who practice NLP evaluate their own and other viewpoints to develop a systematic overview of one circumstances. By understanding a variety of perspectives, the NLP user gains info. Advocates of this school of idea really believe the senses are important for processing available info and that the body and mind influence each other. Neuro-linguistic programming is an experiential approach. Therefore, if a person wants to comprehend an action, they must perform that same action to learn much from the experience.

NLP specialists really believe there are natural hierarchies of learning, communication, and change. The 6 sensible levels of change are:

Purpose and spirituality: This can be participation in something bigger than oneself, such as religious belief, principles, or another system. This is the highest level of change.

Identity: Identity is the person you perceive yourself to be and includes your duties and the roles you play in life.

Beliefs and values: These are your individual belief system and the concerns that matter to you.

Capabilities and skills: These are your abilities and what you can do.

Behaviors: Behaviors are the particular actions you perform.

Environment: Your environment is your context or setting, including any other people around you. This is the most affordable level of change.

The purpose of each rational level is to organize and direct the info below it. As a result, making a change in a lower level may trigger changes in a greater level. However, making a change in a greater level will also lead to changes in the lower levels, according to NLP theory.

NEURO-LINGUISTIC PROGRAMMING IN TREATMENT.

A core idea of NLP can be summarized by the saying, "The map is not the area," since it highlights the distinctions between belief and reality. It points out that each person runs within their own perspectives instead of from a location of neutrality. Proponents of NLP believe everybody's understanding of the world is distorted, restricted, and distinct. A therapist who practices NLP should therefore comprehend how an individual in treatment views their "map" and the impact this understanding might have on that person's ideas and behavior.

An individual's map of the world is formed from data gotten through the senses. This info can be acoustic, visual, olfactory, gustatory, or kinesthetic. NLP practitioners actually believe this info differs individually in regards to quality and importance, and that each person processes experiences using a primary representational system (PRS). For an NLP therapist to work successfully with an individual in treatment, the therapist must attempt to match that person's PRS to use their personal map. NLP specialists actually believe it is possible to access representational systems using hints, like eye motions.

NLP therapists deal with people to understand their thinking and behavioral patterns, emotion, and aspirations. By taking a look at a person's map, the therapist can help them find and strengthen the abilities that serve them best and help them in developing new methods to change ineffective ones. This process can help people in treatment reach treatment goals.

Supporters of NLP claim the method produces fast, enduring results and enhances understanding of cognitive and behavioral patterns. NLP also seeks to build reliable communication between conscious and unconscious psychological procedures to help people increase imagination and analytical abilities. Some advocates of NLP compare the method to cognitive behavior therapy (CBT) but assert positive changes might be made with NLP in less time.

Since its creation, neuro-linguistic programming has been used to deal with a large range of concerns. These consist of:

Stress and anxiety, phobias, and panic.

Communication problems.

Posttraumatic tension.

Depression.

Attention-deficit hyperactivity.

Addiction.

Schizophrenia.

Obsessions and compulsions.

Borderline character.

NEURO-LINGUISTIC PROGRAMMING RESEARCH.

Though limited in number, scientific studies have examined the efficiency of NLP as a treatment technique. In a 2013 research study, scientists investigated whether the language and visualization methods used in neuro-linguistic programming would help children with unique education needs be better prepared for learning in the classroom. Researchers concluded NLP strategies helped the kids develop a positive frame of mind favorable to learning. However, it was also explained that these were "brief, tentative conclusions." In addition to other restricting aspects, the sample consisted of only 7 kids.

NLP professionals claim eye movement can be a trustworthy indication for lie detection. In 2012, scientists tested this claim in a series of three research studies. In the first study, the eye movements of individuals who were telling the truth or lying did not match proposed NLP patterns. In the 2nd research study, one group was outlined the NLP eye movement hypothesis while the control group was not. Nevertheless, there was no considerable difference between both groups after a lie detection test. In the 3rd research study, the eye movements of each group were coded at public press conferences. Again, there was no significant difference in eye movement between them.

An organized evaluation of the effect of NLP on health was carried out by researchers in 2012. In this review, 10 studies resolving issues consisting of drug abuse, anxiety, weight management, morning sickness, and claustrophobia were evaluated. The researchers concluded that while strong proof did not exist of NLP being inefficient, there was little proof to suggest NLP interventions improved health.

ISSUES AND RESTRICTIONS OF NEURO-LINGUISTIC PROGRAMMING EXPLAINED

Due in part to its diverse nature, neuro-linguistic programming is difficult to define as a treatment method. The most substantial constraint of neuro-linguistic programming is probably a lack of empirical proof to support the many major claims made by supporters.

While numerous testimonials praise the approach, there have been couple of scientific research studies to date offering firm, unbiased evidence that it is an effective mode of treatment for mental health problems. NLP co-founder Richard Bandler has often voiced dispute with the scientific testing of NLP.

Furthermore, the lack of regulation in training and certification has resulted in a lot of people becoming NLP professionals in spite of not having trustworthy experience or a background in psychological health.

Why is NLP so questionable?

In psychological treatment, there are a lot of supposed gurus who have created their own healing methods. Some of these supposed experts have created their own techniques with a negative view-- to sell treatments so as to make money. Others of these self-styled professionals may believe that they genuinely are doing great-- even though there is not any clinical evidence to back up their claims.

In 2006, a group of researchers conducted a survey asking 101 psychological health professionals to rank the credibility of some lots apparently psychological therapies. The researchers were led by John Norcross, who got a doctorate in scientific psychology from the University of Rhode Island. At the time of the study, he was a teacher of psychology at the University of Scranton in Philadelphia.

Norcross and his group asked the professionals (who consisted of mainly fellows of the American Psychological Association along with current and previous editors of academic journals in psychological health) to rate the numerous supposed therapies on a scale of 1 (for "not rejected") to 5 (for "certainly discredited"). For instance, there is something called angel therapy, which professionals use to treat mental and behavioural conditions. Angel treatment was rated at 4.98-- as something highly challenged. Past lives therapy for the treatment of psychological or behavioural disorders was ranked at 4.92.

NLP was rated at 3.87. In simple fact, it was rated as more discredited than other therapies like psychiatric therapy for the treatment of penis envy (which received a marginally lower, better rating of 3.52). Even acupuncture for the treatment of psychological and behavioural disorders got a more beneficial (i.e. less discredited) score of 3.49.

University of Sydney researcher Anthony Grant kept in mind that many scientists "argue that NLP is not evidence-based (i.e. there is little peer-reviewed evidence to show that

NLP actually works. The opposite side might then respond that practitioners know that it works since they have personally experienced substantial change in NLP clients."

Most likely even specialists who use angel treatment and past lives treatment really believe that they have personally experienced considerable change through their methods. Nevertheless, some may argue that mere belief without evidence might actually better be viewed as delusion.

How much training do NLP professionals have?

A lot of the commercially readily available programs say that they can accredit people as Master Practitioners in NLP in around 12 to 15 days. Nevertheless, think about that most counselling or scientific psychologists in the UK and US take between 3 to five years to acquire their certifications and certifications.

What is the modern mental view of NLP?

Scientists and qualified psychologists are primarily damning about NLP. In a 2019 paper published in International Coaching Psychology Evaluation, a group of professionals wrote that: "there are lots of critics of NLP who view NLP as variably a pseudoscience, pop psychology or even a cult, without any evidence base for its efficiency."

Based on their own examinations of 90 posts that they found on the topic of NLP, they concluded: "In summary, there are no empirical research studies that provide evidence for the efficiency of coaching based exclusively on NLP tools and strategies."

That is important. They did not find that there were only a few scientific research studies supporting NLP. They found no documents-- absolutely no, zilch, not one.

As just one example, think about a series of examinations led by Richard Wiseman, a professor of psychology at the University of Hertfordshire. NLP contends that people's eye movements can be indicative of their frame of mind or even when they are lying. However, the data gathered by Wiseman and his colleagues led them to conclude: "the actual results of the three research studies fail to support the claims of NLP."

In another recent academic paper, Henley Business School researchers Jonathan Passmore and Tatiana Rowson reviewed the science of NLP and concluded: "we have no doubt in coming to the view that coaching psychologists and those thinking about evidenced based coaching would be smart to neglect the NLP brand in favour of models, methods and strategies where a clear proof base exists."

A different evaluation by Tomasz Witkowski used more powerful language, criticising NLP as "filled with borrowings from science or expressions referring to it, without any scientific meaning. It is seen already in the very name-- neuro-linguistic programming-- which is a terrible deceptiveness. At the neuronal level it supplies no explanation and it has nothing in common with academic linguistics or programming." At the conclusion of his paper, he concluded that: "NLP represents pseudoscientific rubbish, which should be mothballed forever and ever."

Successful seduction begins with who you are and the kind of sexy energy you express. It requires creating yourself, or refining yourself, in one of the seducer categories.

Sirens have a lot of sexual energy and know how to make use of it.

They draw in their targets, like the sirens of Odysseus, through their looks and erotic teases. Crafting the best seductive position for their target.

Rakes insatiably adore the opposite sex, and their desire is transmittable.

Unlike the regular, careful male, the Rake is wonderfully unrestrained, a servant to his love of women. There is the added lure of his track record: so many ladies have succumbed to him, there needs to be a factor.

Keep in mind: it is the form that matters, not the content. The less your targets focus on what you say, and the more on how it makes them feel, the more seductive your impact. Give your words a lofty, spiritual, literary flavor the better to insinuate desire in your unwitting victims.

To play the Rake, the most apparent requirement is the ability to let yourself go, to draw lady into the type of purely sensual moment in which past and future lose meaning. You must have the ability to abandon yourself to the moment.

If no challenges face you, you must create them. Seduction requires some changes.

Suitable Lovers have an aesthetic perceptiveness that they use to love.

Casanova was maybe the most successful seducer in history; few women could resist him. His technique was easy: on meeting woman, he would study her, accompany her state of minds, learn what was really missing in her life, and provide it. He made himself the Suitable Fan.

But attract their better selves, to a higher requirement of beauty, and they will hardly notice that they have been seduced. Make them feel elevated, lofty, spiritual, and your power over them will be unlimited.

Talleyrand simply held up a mirror to Napoleon and let him look that possibility. People are always susceptible to insinuations like this, which stroke their vanity practically everyone's vulnerable point. Mean something for them to desire, expose your faith in some untapped potential you see in them, and you will soon have them eating out of your hand.

Dandies like to have fun with their image, creating a striking and androgynous allure.

The majority of us feel caught within the limited roles that the world expects us to play. We are quickly drawn in to those who are more fluid, more ambiguous, than we are-- those who develop their own persona. Dandies excite us because they cannot be categorized, and hint at a freedom we really want for ourselves.

Dandies seduce socially along with sexually; groups form around them, their style is extremely imitated, an entire court or crowd will fall in love with them. In adapting the Dandy character for your own purposes, remember that the Dandy is by nature a rare and gorgeous flower. Be different in ways in which are both striking and aesthetic, never ever repulsive; poke fun at current patterns and styles, enter an unique direction, and be very withdrawn in what anyone else is doing. Many people are insecure; they will wonder what you depend on, and gradually they will pertain to appreciate and mimic you, as you reveal yourself with total confidence.

Naturals are instinctive and open.

Coquettes are self-sufficient, with an interesting cool at their core.

Coquettes seem totally self-dependent: they do not really need you, they appear to say, and their narcissism shows diabolically appealing.

People are naturally perverse. A simple conquest has a lower value than a challenging one; we are only really excited by what is denied us, by what we cannot have in full. Your greatest power in seduction is your capability to turn away, to make others come after you, delaying their fulfillment.

To comprehend the strange power of the Coquette, you must first understand a crucial property of love and desire: the more obviously you go after a person, the most likely you are to chase them away.

Self-esteem is important in seduction. (Your attitude toward yourself reads by the other person in subtle and unconscious ways.) Low self-confidence repels, confidence and self-sufficiency bring in. The less you appear to need other people, the most likely other ones will be drawn to you.

Charmers want and know how to please-- they are social creatures.

Charmers do not argue or fight with others, grumble, or pester-- what could be more seductive?

First, they don't talk much about themselves, which heightens their mystery and disguises their limitations. Second, they appear to be interested in us, and their interest is so wonderfully focused that we relax and open up to them. Finally Charmers are pleasant to be around. They have none of the majority of people's ugly qualities-- unpleasant, grumbling, self-assertion.

Charismatics have an unusual self-confidence in themselves.

Learn to produce the charismatic illusion by radiating strength while remaining removed.

Creating the air of charisma:

Purpose. If people actually believe you have a strategy, that you know where you are going, they will follow you naturally The direction doesn't matter: select a cause, a perfect, a vision and show that you will not sway from your goal.Mystery. Secret lies at charisma's heart, but it is a specific type of mystery-- a secret uttered by contradiction, by having clashing traits.Saintliness. The majority of us need to compromise constantly to endure; saints do not. They should live out their ideal visions without caring about the effects. The saintly effect bestows charisma.Eloquence. A Charming relies on the power of words.Theatricality. A Charming is larger than life, has additional presence.Uninhibitedness. Most people are quelched, and have little access to their unconscious-- a problem that produces chances for the Charismatic, who can become a sort of screen on which other ones project their secret fantasies and longings.Fervency. You need to really believe in something, and to actually believe in it highly enough for it to stimulate all your gestures and make your eyes light up.Vulnerability. Charismatics display a real need for love and affection.Adventurousness. Charismatics are unconventional.Magnetism. If any physical attribute is crucial in seduction, it is the eyes. They expose excitement, stress, detachment, without a word being spoken.

People do not want to hear that your power originates from years of effort or discipline. They choose to think that it originates from your character, your character, something you were born with.

Stars are heavenly and cover themselves in secret.

People are hopelessly susceptible to myth, so make yourself the hero of a great drama. And keep your range-- let people relate to you without having the ability to touch you. They can only watch and dream.

First, you must have such a large presence that you can fill your target's mind the way a close-up fills the screen.

Second, cultivate a blank, strange face, the center that radiates Starness.

The Anti-Seducer: those who ward off

Anti-Seducers come in tons of shapes and kinds, but nearly all of them share a single quality, the source of their repellence: insecurity.

It is crucial to acknowledge anti-seductive qualities not only in other ones but also in ourselves. Practically all of us have a couple of the Anti-Seducer's qualities latent in our character, and to the degree that we can consciously root them out, we become more seductive.

The Brute: Who has no persistence, who wants to skip the seduction, who offends with egotism.

The Suffocator: Those who stick continuously to you, love you before you know who they are, or who make themselves a doormat to you in their obsession.

The Moralizer: Who wants you to bend to their requirement.

The Tightwad: Cheapness shows more insecurity beyond cash.

The Bumbler: The awkward speaker, who makes other ones feel awkward too.

The Windbag: Who won't shut up.

The Reactor: Who is horrified to have their ego harmed.

The Vulgarian: Who overlooks the rules of the game, presents a garrish image, doesn't play the game and yet expects to win.

It is rather because wordless communication (through clothes, gestures, actions) is the most enjoyable, exciting, and seductive form of language.

The 18 Kinds Of Seducer Victims

Never ever try to seduce your own type.

People are constantly providing signals of what they lack, you need to tune in to these signals and interpret their type based upon them.

The Reformed Rake or Siren: They frantically long to get away whatever confined them in, what is preventing them from being their regular easily sexual self.

The Disappointed Dreamer: They wish for experience, but are stuck in a dull lifestyle.

The Pampered Royal: The long to be swept off their feet by a prince charming and let them live out their fantasy of being spoiled and treated like royalty.

The New Prude: excessively concerned with their external appearance, beneath they want to launch, but they fear judgement. They need to feel like they're sharing some secret with you ...

The Crushed Star: No longer the center of attention, they long to have that sense of being loved back.

The Novive: They want to at least feel that you're somewhat "young" too, but are also excited by the possibility of being introduced to a new, darker world ...

The Conquerer: You need to give them a challenge to overcome, an objective, a goal.

The Exotic Fetishist: They want novelty, new experiences, things on the edge, you need to position yourself as something exotic.

The Drama Queen: They wish for drama in their lives, so you'll really need to help produce it to keep them rapt.

The Professor: They analyze and believe deeply about everything, but long to be overwhelmed by a more free spirit who can help them launch their psychological barrier.

The Appeal: Used to being valued, you must focus on the less complimented functions like her intellect or wit.

The Aging Child: Still immature and desiring an encouraging parent, you must allow their childish desires while still occasionally reeling them in.

The Rescuer: They long to just feel like they're saving someone from themselves, you should make them feel that they can "save" you from something and they will become consumed. Let her be your maternal protector.

The Roué: Experienced in life, they desire to inform someone more naive.

The Idol Worshipper: You must become their thing of worship that provides the meaning in life that they seek.

The Sensualist: Driven by their senses, you need to overwhelm their site, odor, and touch, to totally draw them in.

The Lonely Leader: Act as their equal or superior, the sort of relationship they rarely have.

The Floating Gender: Float with them.

Seduction Stage 1: Separation, Stiring Interest and Desire

Choosing the right victim

The right victims are those for whom you can fill a void, who see in you something exotic.

To leave people who are unattainable to you alone is a wise path; you cannot seduce everybody.

Never hurry into the waiting arms of the first person who appears to like you. That is not seduction but insecurity.

People who are outwardly distant or shy are typically better targets than extroverts. They are passing away to be extracted, and still waters run deep.

On the other hand, you should usually stay away from people who are preoccupied with business or work-- seduction needs attention, and busy people have insufficient space in their minds for you to occupy.

Creating a False Complacency, Technique Indirectly

Once you have chosen the right victim, you must get his or her attention and stir desire. To move from friendship to love can win success without calling attention to itself as a maneuver.

First, your friendly discussions with your targets will bring you valuable information about their characters, their tastes, their weak points, the childhood yearnings that govern their adult behavior.

Second, by hanging around with your targets you can make them comfortable with you.

Then, shock their expectations with an errant touch or tip, make them now interested.

There is nothing more efficient in seduction than making the seduced think that they are the ones doing the seducing.

The first move to master is simple: once you have chosen the right person, you should make the target pertained to you.

Way too much attention early on will actually just suggest insecurity, and raise doubts regarding your motives. Worst of all, it gives your targets no room for creativity. Take a big step back; let the thoughts you are provoking pertained to them as if they were their own.

In all arenas of life, you should never ever give the impression that you are angling for something-- that will raise a resistance that you will never reduce. Learn to approach people from the side.

Send Out Mixed Signals

What is apparent and striking might attract their attention in the beginning, but that attention is usually temporary; in the long run, obscurity is much more powerful. The majority of us are much too obvious-- instead, be hard to figure out.

To deepen their interest, you should hint at an intricacy that cannot be comprehended in a week or more.

If you have a sweet face and an innocent air, let out hints of something dark, even vaguely terrible in your character.

Seem a Things of Desire: Develop Triangles

You see a man alone, whom nobody speak with for any length of time, and who is wandering around without company; isn't there a kind of self-fulfilling seclusion about him? Why is he alone, why is he avoided? There has to be a reason.

When individuals' vanity is at risk, you can make them do whatever you want. According to Stendhal, if there is lady you have an interest in, pay more attention to her sister. That will stir a triangular desire.

Men who really believe that a rakish credibility will make ladies fear or distrust them, and should be played down, are rather really wrong. On the contrary, it makes them more attractive.

Create a real need, stir stress and anxiety and discontent

People are always susceptible to being seduced, since in simple fact everyone lacks a sense of efficiency, feels something missing deep inside. Bring their doubts and stress and anxieties to the surface and they can be led and lured to follow you.

Make people anxious about the future, make them depressed, make them question their identity, make them pick up the monotony that munches at their life. The ground is prepared. The seeds of seduction can be planted.

Master the Art of Insinutation

There is no recognized defense, though, against insinuation-- the art of planting ideas in individuals' minds by dropping elusive hints that settle days later, even appearing to them as their own idea. Make every little thing suggestive.

Enter Their Spirit

Play by their rules, enjoy what they enjoy, adjust yourself to their moods. In doing so you will stroke their deep-rooted narcissism and lower their defenses.

Produce Temptation

As the serpent tempted Eve with the guarantee of forbidden knowledge, you need to awaken a desire in your targets that they cannot manage. Find that weakness of theirs, that dream that has yet to be realized, and tip that you can lead them towards it.

Find that childhood insecurity, that do not have in their life, and you hold the key to tempting them. Their weakness might be greed, vanity, monotony, some deeply quelched desire, an appetite for forbidden fruit. They signal it in little details that elude their conscious control: their style of clothes, an offhand remark.

Stage 2: Lead Astray-- Creating Satisfaction and Confusion

Keep Them In Suspense, what comes next?

Behave in a way that leaves them wondering, What are you approximately? Doing something they do not anticipate from you will provide a delightful sense of spontaneity-- they will not be able to anticipate what comes next.

There are all types of calculated surprises you can spring on your victims-- sending a letter from out of the blue, showing up all of a sudden, taking them to a place they have never ever been. But most importantly are surprises that expose something brand-new about your character.

Reliability is fine for drawing people in, but stay reliable and you stay a bore. Pet Dogs are dependable, a seducer is not.

Use the Demonic Power of Words to Sow Confusion

Inflame individuals' feelings with loaded expressions, flatter them, comfort their insecurities, envelop them in dreams, sweet words, and promises, and not only will they listen to you, they will lose their Will to withstand you.

Lady was beautiful, yet lacked self-confidence in her own wit and intelligence? He made certain to say that he was bewitched not by her beauty but by her mind.

Pay Attention to Detail

Poeticize Your Presence

You can be harmful, naughty, even somewhat vulgar, depending upon the tastes of your victim. But never ever be ordinary or minimal. In poetry (rather than reality), anything is possible.

The only thing that cannot be idealized is mediocrity, but there is absolutely nothing seductive about mediocrity. There is no possible way to seduce without creating some kind of dream and poeticization.

Deactivate Through Strategic Weakness and Vulnerability

The best way to cover your tracks is to make the other person feel superior and stronger. If you seem to be weak, vulnerable, enthralled by the other person, and unable to control yourself, you will make your actions look more natural, less computed.

Remember: what is natural to your character is naturally seductive. An individual's vulnerability, what they seem to be not able to control, is often what is most seductive about them.

Woman, for instance, might be drawn in by a guy's strength and self-confidence, but way too much of it can create worry, seeming abnormal, even ugly.

Confuse Desire and Reality-- The Perfect Illusion

Your task as a seducer is to bring some flesh and blood into someone's dream life by embodying a fantasy figure, or creating a situation looking like that person's dreams.

Separate the Victim

Different them from their environment physically, mentally, and mentally, so they can become further immersed with you.

Stage 3: The Precipice, deepening the impact through severe measures

Prove Yourself

Do not worry about looking silly or slipping up-- any sort of deed that is self-sacrificing and for your targets' sake will so overwhelm their feelings, they will not notice anything else.

Cleverly lead your victim into a situation, a moment of danger, or indirectly put them in an uncomfortable position, and you can play the rescuer, the gallant knight.

Influence a Regression

Stir Up the Transgressive and Taboo

Making your targets feel that you are leading them past either sort of limit is profoundly seductive. People yearn to explore their dark side.

But we are weird animals: the moment any type of limit is imposed, physically or mentally, we are immediately curious. A part of us wants to surpass that limitation, to explore what is prohibited.

The most blatant way to do this is to take part in behavior that gives you a dark and forbidden aura. Theoretically you are someone to avoid; in simple fact you are too sexy to resist.

Use Spiritual Lures

Everybody has doubts and insecurities-- about their body, their self-worth, their sexuality. If your seduction appeals solely to the physical, you will stimulate these doubts and make your targets uneasy. Instead, lure them out of their insecurities by making them concentrate on something superb and spiritual: a spiritual experience, a lofty masterpiece, the occult.

Mix Pleasure with Strong pain

Entice them in with concentrated attention, then change direction, appearing unexpectedly uninterested. Make them feel guilty and insecure. Even initiate a break-up, subjecting them to an emptiness and strong pain that will give you room to maneuver

Your seduction should never follow a simple course up towards enjoyment and harmony. The climax will come prematurely, and the pleasure will be weak. What makes us intensely really appreciate something is former suffering.

Without tension, without anxiety and thriller, there can be no sensation of release, of real satisfaction and pleasure. It is your task to produce that stress in the target, to stimulate feelings of anxiety, to lead them to and fro, so that the conclusion of the seduction has real weight and intensity. So rid yourself of your nasty practice of avoiding conflict, which is in any case unnatural. You are usually nice not out of your own inner goodness but out of worry of upseting, out of insecurity.

Stage 4: Move in for the kill

Give Them Space to Fall-- The Pursuer Is Pursued

Stir the pot by appearing interested in another person. Make none of the specific; let them only notice it and their imagination will do the rest, creating the doubt you prefer.

Understand this: an individual's willpower is straight linked to their libido, their sexual desire. When your victims are passively waiting for you, their sexual level is low. When they turn pursuer, getting involved in the procedure, teeming with stress and anxiety, the temperature is raised.

Apply Physical Lures

While your cool, nonchalant air is calming their minds and decreasing their inhibitions, your glances, voice, and bearing-- oozing sex and desire-- are getting under their skin, annoying their senses and raising their temperature.

Second, look out to the signs of physical excitation. Blushing, trembling of the voice, tears, unusually powerful laughter, unwinding movements of the body (any kind of uncontrolled mirroring, their gestures imitating yours), a revealing slip of the tongue-- these are indications that the victim is slipping into the moment and pressure is to be used.

Master the Art of the Bold Move

Someone must go on the offensive, and it is you.

Be aware of the Side effects

Stir the pot, even if that means a return to causing real pain and drawing back. Never ever depend on your physical beauties; even beauty loses its appeal with repetitive exposure. Only technique and effort will battle inertia

Keep your secret and lightness

Stay away from the slow burnout, Once you feel disenchanted and know it is over, end it rapidly, without apology. Once you are truly disenchanted, there is no going back, so do not hang on out of false pity. It is more thoughtful to make a tidy break. If that seems inappropriate or too ugly, then deliberately disenchant the victim with anti-seductive behavior.

Sex-traffickers hunt for victims outside large group houses filled with foster kids who have been abandoned by their families and near high schools because "victimization is all about vulnerability," says Laura Riso, a victim's expert with the FBI.

As tons of as 90 percent of sex-trafficking victims suffer abuse-- psychological, physical, sexual-- long before they are forced onto the streets to sell themselves, and traffickers know and make use of the damage that such trauma can trigger, she told The Post.

The traffickers "will try every little thing. It's extremely simple, it's very simple. 'Hey you're truly gorgeous, I love your hair. Why don't you let me take you to dinner?'" Riso said.

Rachel Lloyd, the founder and executive director of the anti-sex-trafficking group Girls Educational & Mentoring Service, added, "There's that appeal of being wanted and being loved. ... [When] someone occurs who can use that, it's extremely compelling, it's extremely easy to get connected into somebody who's promising them the world."

Still, it's not as if sex-traffickers rip the kids off the walkway and take them to a dungeon and chain them up, the experts said-- at least not most of the time anyhow. Pimps use time to groom their victims, flatter them, make them believe they really love them until they're close enough to make their move, they said.

" The method is to try and put their arm around them and get their trust and give them a place to stay and make it appear somebody actually cares about them," Manhattan District Attorney Cyrus Vance explained. It's about "taking kids who require aid, preying upon that need, developing a relationship and then turning against them and turning them into kids who are generating income for them on the street."

Erin Williamson from the anti-trafficking company Love 146 said social media is a common tool for pimps to use to target vulnerable kids.

" The web has made every child online susceptible and available to traffickers ... so a ton of youth are being recruited right from their own home," said Williamson, who has been working on concerns related to kid sex exploitation for the past 20 years.

" It can be a person who is on Facebook and is friend-requesting all of the students who say they go to a specific middle school. And after that when one or two accept, they friend-request all of their good friends and so on. ... By the time they're friend-requesting a susceptible youth, they have 30 mutual friends, and they seem that they're legitimate."

Studies have revealed that the average age of entry into the sex industry is as young as 12 years of age.

The children "are really looking for some type of attachment, some type of caregiver," Williamson said.

" A trafficker comes and says, 'You know, you're more fully grown than other youth your age, there's something special about you, tell me about your goals, who do you want to be.' They spend this time getting to know them, and there's no other way for that youth to know this is all part of the grooming process. It's all done to make the youth feel special. [The traffickers] spend time making connections with them in order to exploit them in the future."

Once the exploitation begins, pimps and traffickers use a cycle of abuse and affection to keep their victims in their clutches and to basically brainwash them into thinking this is the best circumstances for them and most of all, keep them loyal so they won't testify against them to authorities.

" It's a mind game," Riso said.

" [Traffickers will] drive home, 'The Lord don't care about you, Joe don't care about you, only Daddy' ... It's breaking down and reprogramming some of these kids."

So when the police officers do come knocking, the majority of kids have 2 middle fingers in the air and aren't interested in complying with law enforcement, Riso said. This is largely as a result of a psychological impact that happens between a victim and their abuser referred to as a "trauma bond."

Dr. Elizabeth Hopper, who is the director of the anti-trafficking program Project Reach, is a medical psychologist with a background in traumatic tension.

She said four things are normally present when injury bonds happen: The victim must view a very real danger of death and an inability to leave; they must be isolated; and there must be some perception of kindness.

It's the same mindset that keeps battered women with their abusive husbands for many years, and it was notoriously shown by Elizabeth Smart during her 2002 kidnapping when authorities tried to rescue her and she lied about who she was.

Barbara Amaya, 61, was trafficked between the ages of 12 and 24 after she fled from home and was sold to a pimp who brought her to New york city City. Amaya, who details her story in her memoir "Nobody's Girl," said her "injury bond" began with her pimp the first night she met him throughout an automobile trip from Washington, DC, to New york city City quickly after she was sold to him.

"I went to change the automobile radio, and he slapped my hand away, and I was shocked," she said. "I hadn't experienced that with anyone, and then he ensured I saw he had a weapon in his belt.

" He was making sure all these things were in place. [Then] he began asking me en route there, 'tell me what took place in your home,' he came off as my protector, like he was going to help me and love me."

Amaya, who said she had been sexually abused by her dad and her brother, explained that her vulnerability made her an easy target for traffickers.

" For me as a mistreated child of 12, bringing the trafficker cash money each night after being raped by 10 to 20 guys, seeing that I made him, the trafficker, happy, was the exact same as getting an A on a school report," Amaya said. "The human brain doesn't separate. All the brain knows is, 'Wow, I made this person happy. Now I feel happy, too.' "

Williamson said he has seen example after example of injury bonds that are heartbreaking to witness.

" We'll have youth that say, 'I know that he loves me,' and we'll say, 'He literally put a rope around your neck and tried to kill you.' ... And then they'll say, 'Well, he didn't kill me,' so in their mind they really love them. ... In some cases they'll say, 'When I was sick, he went and got me soup and medication. I'm 16 and my own mom has never ever done that for me.' "

Hopper said this phenomenon is often not comprehended by the public and even by some company, triggering them to unnecessarily see victims in a negative light.

"When they just look at the realities of what this person did to you, he made all this cash, he sexually attacked you, he beat you up, he threatened to kill your family, why do you feel this is love? It's quite crucial to enter what it is about that feels like love," Hopper said.

She added that those who escape "the life" often experience serious psychological injury that in some cases lasts several years. But, that's not to say the situation is helpless.

If you like my book, please leave a review. I would appreciate it a lot. Thanks!